Home

Sweet

DYSFUNCTIONAL

Home

Hope for crazy, messed up families

DR. MARK SMITH
AND PASTOR MARK HOLMEN

WHAT OTHERS ARE SAYING

Dr. Mark Smith has done a great job breaking down the story of Jacob. His concise and scriptural explanation pulls together the hidden meanings of the stories we grew up with back in the flannel graphs days. With the addition of Pastor Mark Holmen's comments and discussion questions, families have a great way to sit down and overlay their own stories onto the biblical story of Jacob. As you read deeper into the book you realize, like Jacob's family, every family has their own baggage. What they have shared through this book is that with the help of God, that baggage can be transformed into blessings, and each of us can be transformed by the healing power of God into families of faith! I would recommend this book for use in family devotionals, bible classes, or even personal reflection.

Jack Hardcastle, Family Minister
Hillcrest Church of Christ

Home Sweet Dysfunctional Home
Hope for crazy, messed up families

Copyright © 2014

ISBN: 978-1-935256-50-2

L'Edge Press
PO Box 1652
Boone, NC 28607
ledgepress.com
ledgepress@gmail.com

Home Sweet Dysfunctional *Home is dedicated to my biggest fans*
My wife Sherri
My daughter Abby and her husband Justus
My Son Adam and his wife Ashlynn

TABLE OF CONTENTS

FORWARD
Dr. Mark Smith

I have been a follower of Jesus Christ for about forty-two years, in ministry for over twenty-three years, and an avid Bible reader most of my adult life. One of the things I love most about Scripture is how honest and revealing it is about the people in the Old and New Testaments. I love to read about the lives of men like Noah, Abraham, Moses, David, Elijah, Jeremiah, Peter, and Paul. Of course they had their struggles with sin, as we all do, but God used them in mighty ways despite their many flaws. In the same way I enjoy exploring the lives of women like Miriam, Rahab, Ruth, Hannah, Ester, Mary, Anna, and Lydia. They too had their problems with faithfulness; however, the Lord used them in extraordinary ways. That's why when I read about the lives of these impressive ancient characters, warts and all, I am comforted in knowing that even with my own imperfections there is hope for me as well.

I am sure you could add several more names to the list above who encourage and challenge you to live a more godly life. However, let me get you to think outside the box for a moment. There are several people in Scripture that with the mention of their names in the context of being role models would cause you to laugh-out-loud (LOL). In that case, allow me to throw out the name of a man that would probably be the last person you would consider. His name is Jacob. There is no Biblical character more lifelike, more relevant, and more like ourselves than the second born grandson of the great patriarch Abraham...Jacob, son of Isaac. Most likely he would not

1

have made your top twenty-five "I Want to Be Like That Guy" list of Bible characters but perhaps you may want to reconsider and give him a second look.

To be fair Jacob may not be someone you're very familiar with since his story is sandwiched between his grandfather Abraham's tremendous faith-filled life on the front end and his dynamic son Joseph who saved the world from starvation on the back end. Jacob also doesn't receive a great deal of attention from many pastors on Sunday mornings but, contrary to popular belief, he has a great deal to offer us when it comes to navigating family issues. Whether you are an expert in theology or a casual reader of Scripture you will find more in common with this one-of- a-kind Old Testament character than you may care to admit.

For instance, are there occasions when you have tension in your home? Jacob had loads of that. Do you live with a workaholic? Jacob's wives sure did. Are there children in your home who act first and think later? This was a regular occurrence at Jacob's house. Does favoritism sometimes become an uninvited guest in your household? This was a constant in Jacob's home. Have you struggled with forgiveness...maybe with a sibling? You're possibly more like Jacob than you think. Do you have extended family members who selfishly think of themselves and take advantage of you? Then welcome to Jacob's world. If you find that Jacob's life even remotely resembles your own, then I'm glad this book is in your hands.

Before you get started with your reading, allow me to explain the layout of the book. Chapter one is a simple introduction to get you ready for the meat of the book. Chapters two through ten are laid out in two parts. I write the first part of each chapter as a running, light hearted, creative commentary of an episode of Jacob's life that involves his interaction with members of his family. Then Pastor Mark Holmen takes over and gives practical, thought-provoking application to the issues presented in the chapter. The final chapter is the most important. It is written to help you realize, understand, and cling to the hope that is only found in God's infallible Word.

Pastor Mark's and my prayer is that the Lord uses Jacob's complicated married and parenting life in a powerful way in your own journey as a spouse and as a mom/dad. But, most importantly, we hope you experience the awesome glory and grace of the Almighty God.

FOOT HOLD
Dr. Mark Smith

Many would find it strange that the story of Jacob begins with a prayer. Before he was conceived, his father Isaac would seek the face of God on behalf of his barren wife, Rebekah. Like many godly couples who want to become parents, Isaac knew the only way to get the answer he desired was to ask the Lord for a miracle. Moses, the writer of the book of Genesis, is not privy to the words Isaac used in his prayer but one thing we know for certain, "Isaac prayed to the LORD on behalf of his wife... the LORD answered his prayer, and his wife Rebekah became pregnant" (Genesis 25:21).

Perhaps from Rebekah's point of view the word "pregnant" is an understatement. Pregnant is what many women would say when they are expecting a child. However, Rebekah wasn't pregnant with one child; she was "PREGNANT" with two very active babies. The Bible says, "The babies jostled each other within her, and she said, 'Why is this happening to me'" (Genesis 25:22a)? In other words, there was a dog fight going on inside her body, and she wanted to know why. This was a legitimate question for a woman who was decorating her first nursery. Rebekah, like her husband, only knew one place to turn for her answer and that was to the Lord. Scripture tells us that "The LORD said to her, 'Two nations are in your womb, and two peoples from within you will be separated; one people will be stronger than the other, and the older will serve the younger'" (Genesis 25:23). God in all His omniscient wisdom gave this mother-to-be more information than she could possibly comprehend. But there was one thing she did know; these two kids in her womb were not getting along very well.

As the pregnancy progressed, the sixty year old Isaac and his wife Rebekah must have enrolled in childbirth classes while they eagerly awaited the arrival of their bundles of joy. Then the Bible says, "When the time came for her to give birth, there were twin boys in her womb. The first to come out was red, and his whole body was like a hairy garment; so they named him Esau. After this, his brother came out with his hand grasping Esau's heel; so he was named Jacob" (Genesis 25:24-26). Our dynamic duo exited the unfriendly confines of their amniotic world only to experience the same tensions in a new, larger environment. This was where it all began.

To commemorate this occasion the new parents would give fitting names to their offspring. Their first little boy would be named Esau because of his hairy, red features. To the other, they would give the name Jacob because of the firm grip he had on his brother's heel during birth. The name Jacob literally means "one who grabs the heel" or better translated, "one who trips up." As we will see, the meaning to his name will be an unbelievable foreshadowing of the future events of his life.

The Bible skips ahead in our peculiar pair's lives and points out that "The boys grew up, and Esau became a skillful hunter, a man of the open country, while Jacob was content to stay at home among the tents. Isaac, who had a taste for wild game, loved Esau, but Rebekah loved Jacob" (Genesis 25:27-28). There is not much worth noting in particular about the first part of these verses but the second verse is another story altogether. Somehow the favoritism monster had unexpectedly reared it's ugly head in their home. Isaac and Rebekah should have known better than to allow such a dreadful thing to happen. Weren't the questions of the pre-birth womb-wrestling match and the strange heel grab at their births big enough warning signs? Did they not think that there could be trouble on the horizon between these two ferocious twins? Given their predispositions, didn't they know that their parental bias would draw deep lines in the sand between Jacob and Esau? As expected, the cloud of favoritism that Isaac and Rebekah allowed to shroud their home would earn them a special sign on the front door of their house. A sign that would read: "Home Sweet Dysfunctional Home." Unfortunately, their home would also be the perfect place and environment to foster Jacob's "it's-all-about-me" attitude. An attitude that would follow him for most of his life.

Jacob would grow up and live up to the meaning of his name. The "heel- grabbing, it's-all-about-me, trip-up artist" would soon make a play on his brother to swindle him out of his birthright. The Bible describes the story. "Once when Jacob was cooking some stew, Esau came in from the open country, famished. He said to Jacob, 'Quick, let me have some of that red stew! I'm famished!' Jacob replied, 'First sell me your birthright.' 'Look, I am about to die,' Esau said. 'What good is the birthright to me?' But Jacob said, 'Swear to me first.' So he swore an oath to him, selling his birthright to Jacob. Then Jacob gave Esau some bread and some lentil stew. He ate and drank, and then got up and left. So Esau despised his birthright" (Genesis 25:29-34).

Now with the birthright tightly in his hand Jacob only lacked one thing to make his life complete. He had his sights set on the coveted, family blessing. But to get it would require him to convince his father to give him the blessing instead of his brother Esau. Since Jacob was not the oldest nor the favorite son, obtaining the big prize "by the book" would be impossible.

As Isaac grew older, he knew it was time to pass down the family blessing to his oldest and favorite son Esau. He would give the same blessing that was passed down to him by his father, Abraham. Isaac summoned his beloved son into his tent to request a feast before he would give him the crown jewel of the family. As Isaac was placing his order for dinner, he was unaware that there was a set of ears right outside his tent. His wife, Rebekah, was listening and scheming an alternative plan. Only wanting the best for her baby, she has a brilliant idea to usurp her husband's authority and land her favorite son, Jacob, the blessing she knew was rightfully his. Rebekah told her son, "Go out to the flock and bring me two choice young goats, so I can prepare some tasty food for your father, just the way he likes it. Then take it to your father to eat, so that he may give you his blessing before he dies" (Genesis 27:9-10). Even though there were a few hairy and smelly obstacles to overcome, Jacob and his mom were ready to execute their scam.

Before Jacob would enter his father's tent, he had a few last-minute costume changes to make. Our unscrupulous mother and son twosome found one of Esau's best polyester suits and make a couple of quick alterations. Next they threw together a matching scarf and glove set made of the finest goat skin money can buy. Leaving no stone unturned, Rebekah and Jacob top off the ensemble with authentic smells de Esau to boot. With the gourmet meal in hand, Jacob was now ready to trick his father so he could get his highly-sought-after treat. The Bible says, "Jacob said to his father, 'I am Esau your firstborn. I have done as you told me. Please sit up and eat some of my game, so that you may give me your blessing.' Isaac asked his son, 'How did you find it so quickly, my son?' 'The LORD your God gave me success,' he replied" (Genesis 27:19-20). Isaac had a suspicion that something was not right. His eyesight may have been weak, but his sense of time was still very sharp. To try to get a handle on the situation, Isaac said to Jacob, "Come near so I can touch you, my son, to know whether you really are my son Esau or not" (Genesis 27:21). Nervously Jacob complied. We are told that, "Jacob went close to his father Isaac, who touched him and said, 'The voice is the voice of Jacob, but the hands are the hands of Esau.' He did not recognize him, for his hands were hairy like those of his brother Esau; so he proceeded to bless him. 'Are you really my son Esau?' he asked. 'I am,' he replied" (Genesis 27:22-24). Convinced for the moment, Isaac proceeded to eat his meal. But before he would pronounce his blessing he wanted to run one last check. Isaac said to the man he thought was Esau, "Come here, my son, and kiss me" (Genesis 27:26). This would be the defining moment. Would their plan fail or succeed? As Jacob came near his father, Isaac had one last test. He used his keen sense of smell to make sure he was not being deceived. As Jacob kissed him, his father relaxed and gladly gave Jacob the one thing he had waited so long to give...the family blessing.

After Jacob finished his award-winning, acting debut, it was time to get out of the house before the real Esau came back home. Unfortunately, before Esau could bag some game and bring his tasty food back on a silver platter to his daddy, Rebekah and Jacob had already cleaned up and put away the dishes. They had made fast work out of fooling the nearly blind, old man. The deception was complete. When Esau discovered what had happened, he was livid. He begged his father to give him the blessing too, but his father could not. Isaac had no more blessing to give and sadly was feeling a bit like a goat. In Esau's mind, this was the last straw. He could take it no longer and was ready for revenge. He wanted to kill his little brother, but he would have to wait. The Bible says, "Esau held a grudge against Jacob because of the blessing his father had given him. He said to himself, 'The days of mourning for my father are near; then I will kill my brother Jacob'" (Genesis 27:41). This was a promise he intended to keep.

The scene fades with Rebekah catching wind of Esau's murderous plot and handing Jacob a oneway ticket north to her brother Laban's house until Esau could calm down. That would be the last time Jacob would see his mother. Nonetheless, Jacob had a new start. He made a new life for himself in a new land among new people but, unfortunately, he carried with him some old habits. Because of his upbringing, Jacob let the old lessons he learned back home replay in his life everywhere he went. Since he was exposed to favoritism, he would show favoritism. Since he was accustomed to running away from his problems, Jacob struggled to deal with difficult issues, communication, and conflict. Since he was used to having the upper hand with others, he suffered greatly when people manipulated him. With all he had to battle, possibly the most difficult thing Jacob encountered throughout a large part of his life was his ability to trust God. On several occasions, he found himself attempting to aid the Lord in keeping His Word. But as Jacob struggled through, the Lord never left his side...not for one second. God's grace abounded in spite of Jacob's mistakes and hardheadedness.

We are truly blessed that the Lord has graciously preserved the story of Jacob's life for us in Scripture. Whether you are a husband, wife, parent, or grandparent, God has given us numerous examples through the patriarch's life to teach us how we are and are not to respond to difficult family situations. The Lord also uses Jacob's life to show us the disastrous consequences that can result when we choose to go about life our own way. No matter what we go through in the course of our married life or parenting adventure, there is always hope for our crazy, messed-up families. As we travel in and out of Jacob's life and as we journey through his experiences with his family members, remember one thing: God is giving us a glimpse of a family that is probably not much different than our own.

CATERWAULING
Dr. Mark Smith

It was a homecoming of sorts for Jacob as he arrived in Haran. Although his journey brought him to the home of his ancestors, his arrival to this new and strange land was not because of a scheduled family reunion. Jacob had other reasons for making this journey. As we know, he was on the run from his infuriated twin who wanted him dead. Because of the threat to his life, Jacob decided it was time to skip town.

Being the new kid on the block, Jacob made conversation with the locals to try to get his bearings. After discovering his Uncle Laban was alive and well, the unexpected happened. Out of nowhere a woman, more beautiful and breathtaking than any he had ever seen, walked right into his life. But this was not just any woman; this was Rachel, his uncle's youngest daughter. She was a knockout, and Jacob was head-over-heels in love.

Jacob's long trek was over as he finally made it to Laban's house. While they sat together, Jacob debriefed his uncle and got him up to speed with his situation. "Then Laban said to Jacob, 'Because you are my relative, should you therefore serve me for nothing? Tell me, what should your wages be?' Now Laban had two daughters: the name of the elder was Leah, and the name of the younger was Rachel. Leah's eyes were delicate, but Rachel was beautiful of form and appearance. Now Jacob loved Rachel; so he said, 'I will serve you seven years for Rachel your younger daughter.' And Laban said,

'It is better that I give her to you than that I should give her to another man. Stay with me.' So Jacob served seven years for Rachel, and they seemed only a few days to him because of the love he had for her." (Genesis 29:15-20) Seven years is a long time to wait for anything, but not for Jacob. Once he laid eyes on Rachel, it was love at first sight, and he would do whatever it would take to have her hand in marriage.

Jacob's wedding day must have been filled with joy and excitement, as anyone would expect. Unfortunately, the day after the celebration was the exact opposite. As the sun came up, Jacob awoke with bewilderment and anger as he realized Leah was the woman with whom he had slept, not Rachel. Uncle Laban had pulled the wool over the eyes of the one time deceiver. Jacob demanded an explanation but was only given the runaround about their local custom that the oldest had to be married off first. Leah was his new wife now. Obviously this did not settle well with the new groom; nevertheless, Jacob was ready to renegotiate.

Jacob was back where he started seven years ago, but Laban said, "Finish this daughter's bridal week (Leah); then we will give you the younger one also (Rachel), in return for another seven years of work." (Genesis 29:27). Jacob's fury subsided as he took Laban up on his offer for a second time. It took seven short years and eight long days but, Jacob finally got his bride.

When we look at the first year of this threesome's marriage, we are only given a small amount of information. However Scripture tells us enough to set the stage for the next battle royal. The Bible says, "When the LORD saw that Leah was unloved, He opened her womb;

but Rachel was barren" (Genesis 29:31).

It would be easy to read right past this verse and not give it much thought. But there are two points in this text that would create havoc in Jacob's home for many years to come. These unsuspecting words drew deep lines in the sand between the two wives for the biggest part of their married lives and unfortunately would send shockwaves into the future lives of their children. The Bible says that Leah was unloved and Rachel was loved. Leah was able to conceive and Rachel was barren. This combination put these women in a nasty competition that made life in the home not only awkward but toxic. As each day passed, Leah's and Rachel's relationship spiraled more out of control into a vicious cycle of antagonism toward each other. Each wife of Jacob wanted her husband's attention, love, and devotion. (This was something Rachel had always enjoyed but not Leah.) Leah, being the unloved of the two, concluded that to have a remote chance of Jacob's affections she was going to have to produce a son. Son or no son, Jacob would only give his love to one of the two women. He, of course, chose Rachel but that was not going to stop Leah. Tensions were always high in the newly-formed household of Jacob. Living in a home full of strife can be difficult for every family member. Even with all this drama playing out, within a year the long wait for Jacob to continue the promise made to Abraham was over. The Lord gave him a son.

God had compassion on Leah, and she became pregnant beating her sister to motherhood. The Bible says, "When the Lord saw that Leah was not loved, He enabled her to conceive, but Rachel remained childless" (Genesis 29:31). Later Leah announced, "It is because the Lord has seen my misery. Surely my husband will love me now" (Genesis 29:32). Would this actually turn the tide? Would Jacob start to show some interest and genuine love to Leah? She did give him a son which ought to account for something. But unfortunately it did not. Since Leah would not get the one thing her sister always received (Jacob's love), she would show no mercy of her own. She would name her little boy Reuben. Reuben's name is a play on words which literally means, "look a son." Leah would see to it that his name was going to be a constant reminder to both her husband and his other wife. The name Reuben would always bring to Jacob's mind what only Leah was able to give him. For Rachel, the first son was the prize she was unable to give her husband.

Being born into a family filled with jealousy and strife seems unfair to this small innocent child. He didn't do anything to deserve this nor did he ask for it. Unfortunately this was his reality. Reuben landed right in the middle of a cat fight, a "see who can get pregnant first" competition between his mother and his aunt/step-mother Rachel. (This was not the greatest of starts for Jacob's heir.) But even with all the turmoil swirling around him, Reuben had the brightest future of all the sons of Jacob. Being the first boy of this special family, he would be the successor of the blessing that had been passed down from his great-grandfather Abraham. Firstborn sons had special entitlements. With such a bright outlook on the horizon we would expect Reuben's story to be the model for future fairytales. Unfortunately the script of his life has nothing to do with happy endings. When you consider what is recorded in the book of Genesis, his life's story can better be described as a nightmare from start to finish. To put it bluntly, Reuben was center stage with the spotlight directly on him but was never able to stay in character.

As it so happens, when Reuben was a little boy, he started his day like most days as a five-year-old living in Haran. He was outside in the fields. Whether he was working in the fields helping to bring in the harvest or just hanging around where all the action was taking place, we're not told. Whatever the case, Reuben was in the right place at the right time. The Bible tells us, "During wheat harvest, Reuben went out into the fields and found some mandrake plants, which he brought to his mother Leah" (Genesis 30:14a). Back then people superstitiously thought this rare plant was an aphrodisiac. This meant that in the hands of Jacob's two wives mandrakes were a valuable commodity. Leah, who was unloved and rarely enjoyed any intimacy with Jacob, had something to use as a bargaining chip in her feud with her sister over her husband's time and attention. On the other hand, Rachel, who was childless, assumed she could use the mandrakes to increase her chances of getting pregnant. These two women were bent on getting what their hearts longed for. They were willing to go to any expense to have what they wanted even if it meant using Reuben as a pawn in their chess match.

As the little farmer brings in his personal yield, Rachel notices Reuben's offering to his mother looks nothing like wheat. She knows immediately what these 'love apples' are and asks her sister for her little boy's findings. Rachel says to Leah, "Please give me some of your son's mandrakes" (Genesis 30:14b). This question seemed to be straight-forward, but Leah did not take it that way. She took Rachel's appeal as a selfish desire. Leah snapped back and said, "Wasn't it enough that you took away my husband? Will you take my son's mandrakes too" (Genesis 30:15a)? What seemed to be a simple request to share Reuben's unique plant discovery had now turned into a harsh accusation of thievery and greed. Was Rachel

17

out of line with her request or was Leah overreacting? Was Rachel just misunderstood or did Leah actually reveal her own issues with selfishness and greed? Based on Rachel's response these are legitimate questions that demand answers. The Lord may not give us every detail we would like to know from this story, but we do get a clear idea of what was transpiring. We find from Scripture the heart of the issue in one statement. Leah got to hear the one thing she had been desiring. Her sister blurted out, "Very well," Rachel said, "he can sleep with you tonight in return for your son's mandrakes" (Genesis 30:15b). Leah quickly agreed, and the deal was made. However the unfortunate part of the whole bartering process was what was happening to the one who was standing just below eye level. There was an innocent five-year-old with dirty hands and his arms full of mandrakes caught in the crossfire.

In this story we may find ourselves dealing with a range of emotions. To sort them out, let's ask ourselves a few questions. Do we feel sorry for Jacob who was being put up for auction for his male services? Probably we do not, since he was the one who insisted on a second marriage that started this whole mess in the first place. Does anger and rage well up inside of us toward the two sisters? Most likely. They were both only thinking of themselves. Leah and Rachel had absolutely no concern for what their bargaining insinuated about their relationship with their husband, nor did they care anything about the rippling effects their narcissistic drama would have in the lives of their children. We are left looking at Reuben. Our hearts go out to this little boy holding the strange-looking plants, and rightly so. At a very early age, Reuben was exposed to living conditions that were dismal, deranged, and dysfunctional. Sadly this unstable home environment made for an unnecessarily difficult and wearisome childhood for Jacob's firstborn son.

LET'S GET PRACTICAL
Pastor Mark Holmen

I don't know about you, but there are a lot of things I find disturbing in this story. There is Jacob's desire for his uncle's daughter which is incest that is not only committed once but twice as he ends up marrying both of his uncle's daughters! Then you have the whole situation where a husband has two wives and he clearly loves one while simply putting up with the other. And finally you have God intervening into this messy situation allowing one wife to get pregnant while preventing the other from getting pregnant. In many ways this looks a lot more like a modern reality TV show that disgusts us, yet we still can't keep ourselves from watching it. Why? Because we want to see what is going to happen next. And usually what happens next doesn't surprise us as we could pretty much predict that things were not going to turn out well.

So what is the point of this story? For me there are several points. Incest is wrong, and marrying two wives is not a good idea especially when you only love one of them. So don't commit incest, and only marry the one you are in love with! Not bad advice and yet there is another lesson from this story which is the greater point. Messy, unstable home environments produce messy, unstable children. Reuben was raised in a very messy, unstable home environment where he was constantly stuck in the middle. As a result he became a very messy, unstable adult who could never seem to get a grip on life as we will discover in the chapters to come.

As a former youth and family pastor, as well as a senior pastor, who had the opportunity to serve literally thousands of people, I can say without question that behind almost every messed-up, unstable adult was some sort of messed-up, unstable home environment. Now don't get me wrong; there are always exceptions to the rule. The majority of adults to whom I ministered who could never seem to get a grip on life were raised in messy, unstable home environments. We live in an age in which we expect everyone else to take care of things for us including our kids. We expect the teachers to teach our kids, coaches to coach them, mentors to mentor them, counselors to counsel them and the church to raise them spiritually. Yet we can't understand when this doesn't work. But the home environment is more influential than anything else when it comes to determining who your child will be.

I spent twenty years working in inner-city ministry, and I encountered many messed-up, inner-city kids. But I also encountered many un-believably-strong, inner-city kids who not only made it but went on to become strong, healthy, faithful and committed leaders in their homes, families and places of work. What was the difference? The kids who were strong and healthy had a strong and healthy home environment. In many cases, it wasn't anything more than a one bedroom apartment in a high rise and yet it was a strong and healthy environment because the mom made sure it was. Many times, even though my home was way bigger and had more things, I found myself jealous of the home environments many of these kids had because it was so safe, understanding, caring and supportive.

LET'S TALK

Here are some questions I would like you to ponder and/or discuss:

1. What kind of home environment have you created for your children?

2. How did the home environment you were raised in shape you both negatively and positively?

3. What can you take from that experience and bring into your home environment, and what can you make sure doesn't happen?

4. Are you spending as much time, energy and resources as you should on making sure things at home are healthy and strong?

5. What changes could you make so that your home environment is more stable and healthy?

Please know that there is no such thing as a perfect family and there is no such thing as a perfect home environment. All of our homes are imperfect and have room for improvement, but its how we handle our imperfections that matter. Do we ignore them and pretend they don't exist and just expect that somehow our kids will turn out okay in spite of these bad home environments? Or do we acknowledge our "issues" at home and work together to get better? Both directions and decisions will influence our children. Not addressing imperfections will produce children who do not address their issues which lead to lifelong frustrations and problems. Addressing our imperfections by growing and evolving to be healthier will produce children who address their issues in life and grow to be healthier through them. Which pathway do you want to put your children on? What you do at home matters.

OCCUPATIONAL HAZARD
Dr. Mark Smith

Shortly after God spoke the heavens and the earth into existence, He created a four letter word that many don't like to hear: work. Work was not an arbitrary thought or something God dreamed up to pass the time away; the Lord had a purpose. Originally, work had nothing to do with painful toil or sweat on anyone's brow. God invented work for us to be productive, to give us an opportunity to be creative like Him, to allow us the satisfaction of accomplishment, and to give us another way of worshipping His greatness. Scripture tells us that "The Lord God took the man and put him in the Garden of Eden to work it and take care of it" (Genesis 2:15). God's goal was for man to use his ingenuity in the Garden and enjoy Him forever. He wanted work to be an expression of creativity and a vehicle to connect with Him. Things were very good in Paradise.

With everything in its place and operating exactly as planned, the Lord gave Adam six days each week to worship Him in this extraordinary way but set the seventh day aside for something special. God would make this one day a more intimate time of communion with His creation. However, sin entered the picture and everything changed. With one bite of the forbidden fruit, Paradise would be permanently off-limits. Because of Adam's disobedience God cursed the ground and then said, "through painful toil you will eat food from it all the days of your life. It will produce thorns and thistles for you, and you will eat the plants of the field. By the sweat of your brow you will eat your food until you return to the ground, since from it you were taken;

25

for dust you are and to dust you will return" (Genesis 3:17b-19). For Adam and throughout the rest of human history, work would never be the same. Work would have traces of productivity, creativity, satisfaction, and worship; but it would only be a shadow of its' original intent. From this point forward, work would be tainted by sin and defined using words like: grind, exertion, sweat, effort, labor, and toil.

Ever since man's exit from the Garden of Eden, people have come to grips with work and, strangely enough, have become friends with this morphed product of the fall. As with most relationships there are some ups and downs; nevertheless, work has remained a constant companion in our daily lives. But there has been one subtle element of work that has slowly crept in and eroded away the fabric of family life. As a result of sin, man has taken work and made it into something that the Creator never intended it to be. For many people what was once designed to be an expression has become an obsession.

Work was no stranger to Jacob and was a healthy part of his life. He honored the Lord with his commitment and ethic. However, there was a season in his life that was vastly different. Jacob, a man who could ill afford another distraction, was lured away from his family and succumbed to the enticement of work's inconspicuous charm. At an important time in his young family's growth and development, Jacob buried himself in the family business.

After he had completed his work detail for Laban, Jacob started toying with the idea of relocating his family. He had spent the last fourteen years away from home, and his family had grown substantially. He now had four wives and twelve children and felt it was time to get back where he belonged, but his father in-law had other plans.

Laban, who didn't want to lose his best farmhand, dangled a carrot in front of Jacob's face. Knowing that Jacob was poured out of the same mold he was, Laban used his son in- law's tendency of "always looking out for number one" to his advantage. Laban enticed him by saying, "Name your wages, and I will pay them" (Genesis 30:28). This statement was an offer Jacob found hard to refuse.

Laban's proposition must have weighed heavily on Jacob's mind. Jacob could have been thinking that if he stayed it could be a way for him to pad his bank account in hopes that when he returned home the Promised Land Daily News would run the headline: "Jacob Makes It Big: Hometown Boy Goes From Rags to Riches." Then again, maybe he wasn't quite ready for a family reunion with his brother yet. Jacob may have envisioned seeing his brother Esau standing at the Promised Land Welcome Center as he and his family approached the city limits and realized the time wasn't right. On the other hand, staying could mean having the chance of getting back at his father in-law for all the years he had worked so hard and had so little monetarily to show for it.

Whether his motivation was money, fear, or revenge, Jacob knew it would be a long and difficult journey back to the Promised Land so potentially going back home with a big wad of dough in his pocket was icing on the cake. Besides Jacob knew his way around the barnyard and was confident he could succeed as a herdsman, but his gain would present other problems.

Laban would ask a second time, "'What shall I give you?' he asked. 'Don't give me anything,' Jacob replied. 'But if you will do this one thing for me, I will go on tending your flocks and watching over them:

Let me go through all your flocks today and remove from them every speckled or spotted sheep, every dark-colored lamb and every spotted or speckled goat. They will be my wages'" (Genesis 30:31-32). Laban probably had to pick his teeth up off the ground. This was a dream come true and a deal he would not pass up. On the flip side, what was Jacob thinking? Wasn't he tired of getting his lunch money taken by that bully Laban? After they shook hands Laban secretly hid all the multicolored and off-colored livestock Jacob thought he would acquire. As it turns out, our duped prince had to start building his portfolio from scratch. When Jacob clocked in the next day he looked at Laban's flocks and all there was to see was black or white animals. Realizing what Laban had done to him again, Jacob was determined and driven to get to work. He rolled up his sleeves and began executing his peculiar business plan. Jacob "took fresh-cut branches from poplar, almond, and plane trees and made white stripes on them by peeling the bark and exposing the white inner wood of the branches. Then he placed the peeled branches in all the watering troughs, so that they would be directly in front of the flocks when they came to drink. When the flocks were in heat and came to drink, they mated in front of the branches. And they bore young that were streaked or speckled or spotted. Jacob set apart the young of the flock by themselves but made the rest face the streaked and dark-colored animals that belonged to Laban" (Genesis 30:37-40). In no time Jacob became a wealthy man and "grew exceedingly prosperous and came to own large flocks, and female and male servants, and camels and donkeys" (Genesis 30:43).

As unorthodox as his methods sound, we have to give Jacob a lot of credit because his plan worked brilliantly. Or do we? What was the real key to his success? Perhaps it was his cutting-edge knowledge in the science of animal breeding and genetics. It could have been all the time he spent in the chemistry lab testing the reaction of poplar, almond, and plane tree limbs mixed with water that helped him discover an animal aphrodisiac. Better yet, maybe it was Jacob's theory that when an animal saw the branches in the water troughs that it imprinted a mental image of spots and streaks in their minds. Then, when the animals mated, they would produce offspring that were also spotted and/or streaked. No, no, and not at all. So what is the answer to his success? Jacob gives us the real answer when he was having a chat with his wives. He told them, "God has taken away your father's livestock and has given them to me" (Genesis 31:9). In other words, Jacob's success was God's doing. It was all His hand and His provision...not Jacob's hand at all.

However, there is still one thing that sticks out in this story that is left unanswered. Why did Jacob go to all the trouble of cutting limbs, peeling bark, and giving the sticks and livestock special arrangement in and around the watering hole? Was Jacob clearing some land and needed to use the timber? Did he think he was adding a unique ambiance to their otherwise dull drinking experience? Or had the Lord given him these instructions? Again no, no, and no way! When we return to the same conversation with Jacob and his wives, God had told him in a dream, "Look up and see that all the male goats mating with the flock are streaked, speckled or spotted, for I have seen all that Laban has been doing to you" (Genesis 31:12). Notice that the streaked, speckled, and spotted animals were mating with only their streaked, speckled, and spotted counterparts. It's also worth noting that God made no mention of limbs, bark, or the needless work required to get the lumber and livestock into place. So what's with all of Jacob's added labor, especially when it was God doing all the work? Even though God was handing him his wealth on a silver platter, Jacob had the insatiable desire to assist God to make sure this business venture worked out to his advantage. Jacob's entire life revolved around being an expert manipulator which constantly resulted in harder and unnecessary work for him. Even with God showing Himself as Jehovah- Jireh (God our provider), Jacob refused to rest in His abundance. This was a foreign concept he found hard to wrap his brain around.

When we take a leisurely glance at this episode in Jacob's life, it's easy to say that the ends justify the means. Jacob works hard, gets back at Laban, sees God's hand at work in his own life, and becomes filthy rich in the process. As true as these statements are, there's another side of this chapter of Jacob's life to consider. Jacob appeared to have it all together as a herdsman, and externally life was improving. But when you look below the surface, his home was a disaster. Every day when he went home, his house was full of turmoil, strife, and negativity. His wives were jealous of one another and constantly at each other's throats. There were a dozen children, all under the age of 7, who were the innocent bystanders of feuding mothers and an absentee dad. Was this an inviting environment? No, not by a long shot, but it was what God had given him. The Lord expected Jacob to be faithful and strive to be a godly husband and parent regardless of the circumstances.

If God was behind Jacob getting his face on the cover of "Forbes Magazine" why did he spend so much time doing extra work? The answer is quite simple. It appears that since home was so chaotic, work became a more favorable companion. Jacob was coaxed away from his family and fell into the arms of work's dark seduction. At an important and critical time in his young children's lives, Jacob immersed himself in the family business and made work an obsession, not an expression, for six long years. Jacob was a self-centered finagler and, as a result, work was more appealing to him than his family.

At some point or season of our lives we have all been guilty of having an obsession of one kind or another. Whether it be work, hobbies, sports, or any number of activities we can allow ourselves to be selfishly consumed. There are many ways to keep busy, but work is possibly one of the most dangerous of all other infatuations. Because of the financial responsibilities we have to our families, employers, and debtors, everyone has to have a job. But what makes work so treacherous is that it has the ability to satisfy our innate desire to produce, create, and be satisfied. If left unchecked and not properly balanced, the long-term effect of this fascination can be as devastating for us as it was for Jacob.

LET'S GET PRACTICAL
Pastor Mark Holmen

As I read the insights Dr. Smith shared in this chapter, a few things struck me that I would like to delve into a little deeper. He stated, "Work was not an arbitrary thought or something God dreamed up to pass the time away, the Lord had a purpose. Originally, work had nothing to do with painful toil or sweat on anyone's brow. God invented work for us to be productive, to give us an opportunity to be creative like Him, to allow us the satisfaction of accomplishment, and to give us another way of worshipping His greatness. For many people what was once designed to be an expression has become an obsession."

The point Dr. Smith is making in this chapter is so significant that it leads me to ask these questions: What is work to you? Is it painful toil or is it another way of worshipping God's greatness? Is it an expression or an obsession?

As we have read, work was given to us by the Lord as a way of worshipping Him. When we look into the life of Jacob, we see he did not deal well with family issues and made himself unnecessarily busy at his workplace. If we are not careful, we too can easily deceive ourselves into thinking that our temporal careers are places to find significance or, worse yet, places we hide from our family problems. When we find ourselves treating our jobs as places of refuge, we are in danger of making work an obsession. That's why we need to guard against letting work have control in our lives.

Perhaps I look at work in a different way than most people. Instead of a job being an obsession, I see it more as a "calling" from God. Work is a means by which I am called to worship the Lord, what I do to help others, and something that helps me provide for my family's needs. Unfortunately I do not think many people understand work as a calling.

In the past God had called me to be a lawn mower, horse wrangler, camp counselor, Wal-Mart worker, nanny, camp director, youth pastor, youth and family pastor, and senior pastor. I can honestly say I worked very hard in each of those positions, but I never considered any of them to be anything close to painful toil. Instead each job was a joy and a calling from God where He was clearly leading me. As I look back, I can also say the Lord used each job opportunity to prepare me for my next calling. Unfortunately many people think "callings" are only for pastors. That is simply not true. We are all called by God to work which means we are all called to use the gifts He has given us to serve Him. So my question is: are you constantly wiping the sweat off your forehead while you are working or are you following His call and using the gifts He has given you to worship Him?

I have a friend, Tristy, who is a hair stylist and her husband, Bruce, is a cabinet-maker. Each of them are clearly called to these professions. When I'm in need of a haircut, I go to Tristy, and when I need some fine cabinetry work done, I go to Bruce because each of them is clearly called and gifted to do those things. Now don't get me wrong, it's still work to cut hair and make a cabinet. But for Tristy and Bruce cutting hair and making cabinets are their ways of serving and worshipping God. People can see that they are called to these jobs because they have complete joy and peace in the work they are doing and are using the gifts they have been given to serve God and help others. Their work is clearly an expression not an obsession. I'm so thankful for people who are called to be hair stylists and cabinet makers because without them my hair would look awful and my cabinets would be unsteady pieces of furniture with lots of bent nails and duct tape!

If I may get a little more personal, let me ask an even more probing question; what would our kids say work is for us? I wonder how Jacob's children would have answered this question? My guess is they would not have been very positive. We know from Jacob's life that he misused work and was not the husband nor the father he needed to be. For six very important years he avoided being the leader of his home and poured himself into his job rather than intentionally engaging in the lives of his family. The reason I ask these questions is because I have had to answer them for myself recently. As a Faith@ Home missionary, I am convinced, now more than ever, our children need to see their parents as people who are called in their jobs and passionate about their families. I believe that when our children see this truth in our lives it will empower and release them to do the same in their own lives.

My daughter, Malyn, is currently being called to pursue pediatric nursing. It is easy to see this is her calling in life because she loves being in hospitals and enjoys volunteering her time to work in the pediatric department of our local hospital. For her, being in a hospital working with infants isn't work, it's what she loves to do. However, she knows to fulfill this calling she needs to get a college education. To help her pay for school, God has opened doors and called her to work at a retail store at a local outlet mall. While the retail job may not be her lifelong calling, it is helping her to use her gifts and make a little money to go toward her college tuition.

Over the years, as I have pastored, part of my work included making hospital visits. I love to spend time with my daughter so I used to take her along with me. I really enjoyed her company as I would go to visit church members who were sick. Little did I know that by simply doing what God was calling me to do, He was at work shaping and preparing my daughter for her future calling. One of the reasons Malyn knows she is being called into nursing is that she feels very comfortable in a hospital partially because she went with me on all those hospital visits. As a result, I learned a valuable lesson. Having a healthy attitude toward work and deepening love toward family has the potential of greatly influencing the people around us, especially our children.

LET'S TALK

Here are some questions I would like you to ponder and/or discuss:

1. What type of example did your parents set when it came to work? Was it a "call" or "job" for them?

2. When you think of someone who has clearly been called to the work they are doing, who comes to mind?

3. What were some of the "callings" you had in your life? How did they shape and mold you for your current call in life?

4. What is your current attitude towards work? Is it a calling or a painful toil?

5. To what do you think your children are being called with their lives?

Jacob's story has been preserved in Scripture to let us see how crazy and unbalanced our lives can sometimes be. As we read about the drama of his life we can feel at times we are reading our own biography. We should not be ashamed or feel like a failure when we find ourselves struggling with the high demands and pressures of home. There are points in our lives when homelife can get a bit dysfunctional. Without even realizing it, we find ourselves retreating into our jobs just to find some semblance of peace. It is Dr. Smith's and my hope and prayer that you would allow God to transform your thinking, attitude, and heart toward your home and employment. No matter how difficult your family situation is, the Lord can bring healing and new life into every aspect of your life. We all make mistakes, but God is more than capable of picking up all the pieces if we allow Him.

HOMECOMING
Dr. Mark Smith

Jacob and his family were on the last leg of their journey to the Promised Land. The morning sun was just peering over the desert mountain range and heating up the dusty road leading out of Peniel. Jacob, coming off a long, sleepless night of tossing and turning, must have had difficulty staying focused as he was slowly making his way back home. With the sun's rays warming his face, his mind was replaying the events of the last several weeks. It began back at his uncle Laban's house in Haran as he secretly uprooted his entire family and possessions and left town. Not long into their journey they were tracked down like escaped convicts by Laban and his men. He then made numerous accusations that ranged from kidnapping his daughters to stealing his household idols. On top of that experience, Jacob had just spent the whole night wrestling with the Lord and was now walking with a limp. There was a lot on his mind.

As Jacob and his caravan slowly meandered it's way through the countryside, the dreaded moment finally arrived. Jacob lifted his head and saw Esau coming to meet him accompanied by a 400-man, welcoming committee. He must have been overwhelmed with the question, "What have I gotten myself into?" In an instant his mind must have raced back to a time when he and Esau were growing up. He remembered the day he was cooking dinner in the kitchen and his brother came in from a long hunting trip. Scripture tells us, "Esau came in from the open country, famished. He said to Jacob, 'Quick, let me have some of that red stew! I'm famished!' (That is why he

was also called Edom.) Jacob replied, 'First sell me your birthright.'
'Look, I am about to die,' Esau said. 'What good is the birthright to
me?' But Jacob said, 'Swear to me first.' So he swore an oath to
him, selling his birthright to Jacob" (Genesis 25:29-33). With the
increasing sound of the approaching posse snapping him back into
reality, Jacob must have thought, "Why was I so underhanded and
greedy with my brother back then? No one should put a price tag on
a birthright. If I would have acted differently, maybe I wouldn't be in
this predicament right now." With each step he took, his heart must
have pounded progressively harder. As the two paths drew closer to
intersecting, Jacob's mind must have drifted back once again to the
last time he saw his brother. He remembered the fire in Esau's eyes
and the rage in his heart. It was just after a time when his mother
had prompted him to play dress up and secretly pretend to be his
brother. Their goal was simple: steal the family blessing that Isaac
was going to naturally pass down to his favorite elder son, Esau.
Since he was less hairy than his brother, Jacob covered his neck
and arms with the skin of a goat. Then cloaked in Esau's own gar-
ments, he went into his nearly-blind father's tent and set before him
his favorite meal. Their plan worked brilliantly and completely fooled
Isaac. Jacob had not only swindled the birthright from Esau, he was
able to steal his brother's blessing too. But now, it appeared, that his
past had caught up to him.

Looking up to see that the four-hundred-and-one-member mob was
closing in fast, every part of his body must have been set on edge.
As he was reliving his sordid past in that moment, it must have hit
him like a ton of bricks why his anxiety level was off the charts. The
last thing his mother told him as he was running out the door (running
away from his brother who vowed to kill him) was "When your brother

is no longer angry with you and forgets what you did to him, I'll send word for you to come back from there" (Genesis 27:45a). His mother never called.

Shaking the cobwebs loose, Jacob does the only thing he knows to do...panic! Without any hesitation he systematically organizes his family in a holocaust-like fashion. As if he was sending his loved ones to the slaughter, "He put the female servants and their children in front, Leah and her children next, and Rachel and Joseph in the rear" (Genesis 33:2). Clearly this order was typical of Jacob's style. Then, unlike a true heel grabber, he does the unexpected. At the ripe old age of ninety-seven and with an injured hip, Jacob runs to the front of the line and systematically bows down to the ground seven times. Jacob was having a moment. For possibly the first time in his life he was showing humility. Instead of living in the flesh, he was now living in the Spirit. As Esau and his men converged on Jacob's parade, he carefully watched his brother's every move. Then the next verse is possibly one of the greatest verses in the entire Jacob/Esau saga. As Esau's regiment came to a stop, the Bible says, "Esau ran to meet Jacob and embraced him; he threw his arms around his neck and kissed him. And they wept" (Genesis 33:4). Just like the Prodigal Son's father was filled with emotion and ran to wrap his arms around his wayward son, Esau could wait no longer to reunite with his twin bother. All of Jacob's fears and anxieties were wiped away in a matter of seconds. Over twenty years of wondering and worrying were now reduced to nothing. Talk about a homecoming! Both men held and kissed one another as their tears flowed. Each drop of water melted their hard hearts until the two men became one. As the two no longer estranged brothers embraced, the over four hundred and sixteen member congregation watched with joy and amazement.

After the reunited brothers had regained their composure, Esau looked up and noticed the 16 people that were accompanying Jacob. Esau must have had his suspicions and asked for an introduction of the spectators. Jacob was quick to give the credit to the Lord but still with a ceremonial tone said, "They are the children God has graciously given your servant" (Genesis 33:5b). Then, in the order they were given preference, each group presented themselves and bowed down in Jacob-like fashion to their newly-acquainted relative. After the introductions were complete, Esau had yet another inquiry. He asked, "What's the meaning of all these flocks and herds I met?" Jacob again diplomatically replied, "To find favor in your eyes, my lord" (Genesis 33:8).

At this point in the story we need to pause and take note of the two brothers' unique approaches in their quest of seeking reconciliation. Notice Jacob's formality in lining up his family. As if to be assembling his wives and children before a potential firing squad, Jacob put his maidservants and their children in the front, Leah and her children in the middle, and Rachel and Joseph in the rear. It's hard not to notice the favoritism. Then Jacob ripped a page from the 14th century B.C. Egyptian history books by formally bowing seven times as a sign of submission, calling himself "servant" and his brother "lord." Even after an emotional reunion, Jacob was still trying to be politically correct almost to a point of acting and sounding rehearsed. However Esau was the polar opposite. The once-irate sibling was anything but methodical. He was completely unconcerned with proper procedure. Esau had no premeditated script nor did he have a single care about what other people saw or thought. Throwing all caution and custom to the wind, he dismounted his animal and took off running toward Jacob.

No other man of his age and stature would have even thought about responding this way especially in front of his loyal entourage. It was considered highly undignified. But Esau did not care. As far as he was concerned, he was holding nothing back. Esau was without restraint because he simply wanted a right relationship with his brother.

Returning to the narrative, the systematic and casual postures continue between the brothers as Esau asks his final question about the meaning of the herds. Then Jacob, staying in character, quickly replies, "To find favor in your eyes, my lord" (Genesis 33:8b). Jacob is still showing respect and formality toward his brother as he presents him with a peace offering. At first Esau refuses his brother's goodwill by saying, "I already have plenty, my brother. Keep what you have for yourself" (Genesis 33:9), but Jacob is persistent. He had his mind made up and said, "No, please! If I have found favor in your eyes, accept this gift from me. For to see your face is like seeing the face of God, now that you have received me favorably" (Genesis 33:10). Was this his attempt of easing his own guilty conscience for stealing his brother's birthright and blessing or was it his sincere way of sharing God's bounty? I believe Jacob was being sincere. He was showing he would do whatever it took to be reconciled with Esau. He would pay any price to have his brother's forgiveness. He was doing the right thing. Esau acknowledges his brother's heart and graciously accepts Jacob's gift. Then, as a gesture of goodwill, Esau also extended a gift to his brother and family. He said, "Let us be on our way; I'll accompany you" (Genesis 33:12). Jacob refused on the basis that it would slow his brother and his men down. Esau then made another offer by saying, "Then let me leave some of my men with you" (Genesis 33:15a). Again Jacob politely, but in proper form, refused by saying, "Just let me find favor in the eyes of my lord" (Genesis 33:15b). Fortunately Esau maintained an easy-going attitude during their whole encounter. He got the hint, does not take Jacob's rejection personally, and departed from his brother in peace. In the end the brothers' approaches to reconciliation were not important. What is significant is that their different methods worked for them. It's not how they sought reconciliation but that they were determined to make things right between them. Jacob and Esau succeeded.

It's difficult to say exactly why Jacob was so formal and Esau so casual during their encounter. Regardless of their reasons, Jacob and Esau had forgiven one another and their hearts were unmistakably reconciled. They got the job done. Jacob and Esau were, perhaps for the first time in their lives, genuinely brothers. But before we close the story on Jacob's and Esau's reconciliation, we must consider how this event affected the sixteen plus innocent bystanders. Jacob's four wives, twelve children, numerous servants, and even the livestock must have all been impressed by the difference in their leaders' actions and attitude. They may have even wondered if someone had kidnapped Jacob and replaced him with an impostor. Nevertheless, this event had long-lasting effects in all their lives, especially the baby of the family.

As the youngest member of the Jacob delegation, Joseph, from the back of the line, had a perfect view of what true forgiveness and reconciliation was. Joseph, who was probably about seven at the time, may not have had any prior knowledge of the long-lasting feud between his dad and his uncle. He most likely did not understand why there was so much tension in the two brothers' relationship. It's entirely possible that Joseph was totally caught off-guard by the whole ordeal and stood in awe as he watched his father and Esau reunite and reconcile their broken relationship. No matter what was going on in this seven-year-old boy's mind, this event left a deep impression on his life. Joseph saw firsthand how different approaches were used by his father and uncle to bring about reconciliation in their relationship. As it turns out, the whole ordeal would be so penetrating that elements of what the entire family just witnessed would be replayed in their own lives thirty years later.

LET'S GET PRACTICAL
Pastor Mark Holmen

I'm not sure if there is a greater "issue" in families than how forgiveness is handled or not handled. Nothing causes deeper wounds or lasting anguish more than when the ones you love the most hurt or sin against you. And in the same way, nothing seems to destroy families internally more than unreconciled issues where forgiveness has not been sought or granted. If you love and if you sin (two unavoidable things for families) then you are going to need forgiveness to play a prominent role in your family.

Although I deeply loved and admired my dad, I was deeply hurt by him. On numerous occasions because he was a closet alcoholic who had multiple anger outbursts against me when he was in a drunken state. I also hurt my dad with things I said or with the disrespectful way I treated him especially during my rebellious, teenage years. I hurt my mom and sisters when I said or did things that I shouldn't have said or done. There were times they needed me to forgive them. My wife and I have had to repeatedly forgive one another during the twenty-three years of our marriage. (Don't ask who's had to forgive the other more!) I have also had to ask my daughter to forgive me, and she has had to ask for forgiveness. I think you could easily say "there is no way to survive as a family without forgiveness," since we all love and sin, forgiveness is going to be required. And while all families handle forgiveness differently, I think there are some principles we can take out of this story that can help us engage in a healthy form of forgiveness in our families.

Forgiveness Principles

1. When you need to be forgiven, humble yourself and seek forgiveness. Do this sooner than later.

We all know when we make a mistake. Yet isn't it amazing how long it takes before we will humble ourselves and seek forgiveness? We will try to rationalize it or avoid it. We hope it will go away, but it does not. It actually makes the wound deeper. I know a man who was hurt when his in-laws chose not to visit or attend the funeral when his mom was tragically killed in a car accident. His in-laws, with whom he had a loving and respectful relationship, were within driving distance as his mom battled to survive in a hospital, and they did not come to visit. When his mom passed away, to his surprise they did not attend the funeral and only sent a condolence card with a small monetary gift for the memorial fund that had been established in her name. Through the whole ordeal he didn't even receive a phone call. His wife, who obviously loved her parents, tried to rationalize their behavior by saying they didn't want to come and be a distraction. But that idea still did not sit well with him. Not wanting to cause a problem, he decided not to address the issue and never said anything. Everyone tried to move forward, but the husband's pain prevented him from spending any time with his in-laws.

Pretty much every family has some sort of example that has caused, or is continuing to cause, damage to their family. In the Twelve Step program of Alcoholics Anonymous the first step that launches the entire recovery process simply begins by admitting you have a problem and need help. In the same way, the forgiveness process begins when people humble themselves and seek forgiveness. As Christ

47

followers we should be quick to humble ourselves and seek forgiveness when we hurt someone. We should not try to rationalize or avoid the situation. We should be the first to run out in front of the individual and lay ourselves down. We should cry out, "I'm truly sorry. Will you forgive me?"

2. Let your family see you seek forgiveness.

I must confess, a new lesson I took from this story is the importance of letting those who know and love you best be a part of your forgiveness journey. I'm not saying they have to be physically there when you go and seek forgiveness, but I do feel there are two good reasons why you would want to engage your entire family in the forgiveness journey even if you have only sinned against one of them.

a. First of all I feel it is a good testimony and example to everyone when they get to witness and experience forgiveness lived out in front of them. At some point and time the shoe is going to inevitably be on the other foot, and they are going to find themselves in a forgiveness-needed situation. They will be able to draw from your experience.

b. Secondly, I feel it is a good accountability system because now others have witnessed the forgiveness being sought and potentially granted. They will remember how both sides responded. So with a few, close, family witnesses engaged in the process BOTH sides are held accountable for their immediate and longterm actions and behaviors. I feel both Esau and Jacob's actions were affected because Jacob's family, as well as Esau's followers, were there bearing witness to their actions and behaviors. While in most situations forgiveness will be handled between two parties, having extended members of the family engaged in the process can help both sides to arrive at an even better-than-anticipated outcome.

3. Don't predict or predetermine the outcomes.

I love movies and stories where you can't predict the outcome. One thing we must recognize is that when we prepare to seek forgiveness, we need to be sure to do so without predetermining the response. We simply need to humble ourselves, seek forgiveness in a sincere way and leave the response in God's hands. Jacob had no idea what Esau was going to do. His actions even showed that, if anything, he was preparing himself for a much different response. But Jacob simply bowed down, in an absolute posture of humility, and gave himself over to his brother. He left the response to God. Before you go to seek forgiveness, get on your knees before God and ask Him to give you humility. Entrust the response to Him by accepting it no matter what it is.

4. Make amends, and do not repeat the behavior.

I love how the story of Jacob and Esau is not just about forgiveness but also about making amends as a part of the process. Jacob tried to give Esau his flocks, and Esau tried to give Jacob some of his men. Both sides were trying to assure the other, through amends that they made/offered, that their act of forgiveness was sincere. As the statement goes, actions speak louder than words. An aspect of forgiveness needs to go beyond words to actions which show we are truly repentant and willing to do whatever it takes to help make things better. Both Jacob and Esau were showing, through their actions, that they truly wanted to reconcile their relationship. If we want true forgiveness to reign in our homes, our actions must reflect our sincerity to be forgiven. In other words, did I not only ask to be forgiven or did I offer to do some tangible things of significance to help the ones I hurt? One of the most tangible things you can do is to take steps or make changes so that you do not repeat the act or behavior that caused the problem in the first place.

5. Allow time to heal the wounds, but realize scars will remain until Christ returns.

As Esau left, things between Jacob and him were reconciled. Because the wounds had been healed, there was a powerful testimony to all involved in the process. We are not privy to what changed with Esau besides the fact that he went from wanting to kill his brother to hugging and kissing him. But something had clearly changed, and chances are it had a lot to do with time healing those wounds. My dad's behavior during his alcoholism days hurt me and remained open wounds for me until he decided to go and get help. Thankfully after treatment my dad was able to kick his addiction, and he lived alcohol-free for over fifteen years. He had asked us for forgiveness, and it was granted. Going into treatment was the beginning of his making amends, but the wounds he caused were deep and took time to heal for all of us. It was not a quick process, and it was different for each member of the family. And while I could testify that our wounds all healed, we definitely each have been scarred for life as a result of what we experienced. Now please know that scars in and of themselves are not necessarily all bad because they serve as reminders that can keep us from making similar mistakes. For example, I have a scar under my chin from a fall I took while trying to flip off a swing.

Guess what I will never try doing again? So the point I'm trying to make is that we must recognize that the hurt caused in families is going to cause deep wounds that can be healed through forgiveness. Yet those wounds are going to leave scars that will remain until Christ comes and restores us fully into His perfect, blameless, and scarless image. Therefore, instead of pretending these scars do not exist, I encourage families to remain open to acknowledging and talking about their scars because that can prevent them from repeating those behaviors or making those mistakes again. After his recovery, I often told my dad how proud I was of the fact that hewasn't the same dad I had when he was drinking and that I would never want to go back to those days. And every time I said this I could see how much that statement meant to him.

LET'S TALK

Here are some questions I would like you to ponder and/or discuss:

1. What scars or wounds do you have as a result of the family in which you grew up?

2. How did your family handle forgiveness when you were growing up?

3. What is your reaction to the five principles of forgiveness?

4. How does your family deal with forgiveness?

5. What takeaway from this chapter would you like to apply in your family?

COMMUNICATION BREAKDOWN

Dr. Mark Smith

Princess, sweetheart, darling, and precious are all nicknames reserved for special people in our lives. These endearing terms have special significance and meaning when given to the ones we love... especially little girls. Dinah was the daughter of Jacob and Leah and the sister of ten older brothers. As far as we know, Dinah was the only girl born into the family. She was the lone sister surrounded by eleven brothers, four mothers, and one dad. Dinah could be considered the family princess in this large and dysfunctional home.

We first meet Dinah in Genesis 30:21. At the end of a long list of boys being born to Jacob and given meaningful names, Dinah's birth announcement almost seems to get lost in the shuffle. With the grand entrance and announcement of each heir of Jacob, verse 21 comes across as a footnote to the royal genealogy. The Bible says, "Some time later she gave birth to a daughter and named her Dinah" (Genesis 30:21). It's hard to not notice the simplicity of this verse when compared to the additional commentary made by Leah and Rachel as each male child arrived. It appears that Dinah has no real significance to the family. She seems to have no distinct purpose or value in their home. So why does Scripture even mention her name in this long list of the sons of Jacob? Why does God allow the author of Genesis to include her name? The reason is simple. Dinah, as well as any other child God brings onto this planet, does have significance, purpose, and value. With each child conceived, God states, "Before I formed you in the womb I knew you, before you were born I

53

set you apart; I appointed you as a prophet to the nations" (Jeremiah 1:5). This story of the solitary daughter of Jacob particularly shows parents the importance of leading their family intentionally.

Even though Dinah doesn't get much of an introduction, being the lone lady of twelve boys, Scripture has much to say about Jacob's daughter and two of her brothers. These three children of Leah find themselves in one of the most violent accounts in all the Bible. The Lord holds nothing back in describing this horrific story of rape, revenge, and murder. Scripture tells the story of Jacob and his family making the long journey back to Canaan from Paddan Aram. After twenty years of service to his uncle Laban, God let Jacob know it was time for him and his family to relocate. This rather large, motley crew picked up everything they had accumulated and headed for the Promised Land. After a short layover to meet Jacob's brother, the family settled in the hill country of Ephraim near a town named Shechem located about nineteen miles north of Bethel. In this small town lived a man named Hamor who was the leader of the Shechemite people. Hamor had a son, also named Shechem, who was the town's young, dashing prince. One day, unannounced to anyone to whom she was related, Dinah decided to explore this nearby settlement. She "went out to visit the women of the land" (Genesis 34:1), because she wanted to see how the other half lived. Little did she know that while she was getting acquainted and making new friends, she had caught Shechem's eye and become his lustful target. Without any warning, what started out to be an innocent 'go meet the neighbors' suddenly turned tragic. The Bible says that Shechem "saw her, took her, and raped her" (Genesis 34:2b). Words cannot bring to light the horror or the anguish she must have felt. Her innocence was gone forever. Unfortunately the nightmare didn't end for Dinah. After the ruthless defilement of the daughter of Jacob, Shechem decided to kidnap his victim and hold her against her will. What led him to do this act of personal violation we don't really know. However, what happened next seems to come out of left field. Something strange happened in Shechem's heart. He was drawn to Dinah and the Bible says, "he loved the young woman and spoke tenderly to her" (Genesis 34:3). But that's not all. Shechem went to his father and said, "Get me this girl as my wife" (Genesis 34:4b). Unbelievable!

News like this travels fast. Before Hamor could schedule an appointment with the aging patriarch, Jacob heard about his daughter's painful plight, but unfortunately decided to do nothing until his sons got back home with the livestock from the fields. Once home, Dinah's brothers heard the terrible news about their sister. They were shocked and outraged to say the least. As the negotiation for the marriage process began, Hamor and Shechem tried to pull out all the stops. They promised peaceful coexistence between both of their communities. (One big happy family.) Their proposal did not impress Jacob's sons so they gave a counter offer. "They said to them, 'We can't do such a thing; we can't give our sister to a man who is not circumcised. That would be a disgrace to us. We will enter into an agreement with you on one condition only: that you become like us by circumcising all your males. Then we will give you our daughters and take your daughters for ourselves. We'll settle among you and become one people with you. But if you will not agree to be circumcised, we'll take our sister and go'" (Genesis 34:14-17). The counter-offer delighted Hamor and Shechem and they accepted the proposal with no questions asked. From their perspective this was a win-win situation. They must have felt they had just won the lottery. Victory was theirs. But to their surprise in just a few days the tables were

55

turned. Simeon and Levi had revenge in their hearts. The brothers had just deceptively orchestrated a secret scheme to pour out their unbridled fury on the men of Shechem and slaughter them all.

After three days had passed and all the men of Shechem had been circumcised, Simeon and Levi took advantage of their weak physical condition. While all the men were still in pain from their surgical procedure the two brothers "took their swords and attacked the unsuspecting city" (Genesis 34:25b). Simeon and Levi unleashed all their anger and executed their premeditated plan like skilled assassins. After the execution was complete the sons of Jacob plundered the entire town. In the end they had taken their livestock, possessions, women, children, and sister home.

When they arrived home with their spoils the brothers were greeted by their father. What kind of reception would they encounter? What were they expecting? Simeon and Levi masterfully devised and carried out a full-scale attack on the Shechemites who had humiliated their family and defiled their sister. Their revenge and rescue was a complete success. Were they expecting to be embraced by their father and cheered by their mothers and other siblings for their accomplishments? Were they thinking they would come home to a hero's welcome? It's hard to say. We are not told what was going through the minds of Dinah's two brothers, but what we are told was probably not what many would expect. Jacob said to his two boys, "You've made my name stink to high heaven among the people here, these Canaanites and Perizzites. If they decided to gang up on us and attack, as few as we are we wouldn't stand a chance; they'd wipe me and my people right off the map" (Genesis 34:30 The Message).

Based on what Jacob said it doesn't appear that he was glad to see his daughter home safely. There is no indication that he was thrilled his two sons were victorious. Nor does it seem that Jacob was excited that his portfolio was substantially increased either. Instead Jacob was more concerned that their actions would incite a riot from neighboring tribes and that their family could face destruction. As the primary family protector, his thoughts were on the overall welfare of his family. Was this wisdom or worry? The story ends with the father and the sons at an impasse. Simeon and Levi responded to their father and said, "Nobody is going to treat our sister like a whore and get by with it" (Genesis 34:31). Spoken like true warriors, these two brothers were unconcerned with how this action may appear to other nearby clans. Their thoughts were not on political correctness. Their hearts and minds were on their sister and the family reputation.

Whether we realize it or not, God has given us two great gifts in the story of Jacob. The first gift is that no one is documenting our family problems or how we deal with them as parents and printing them for everyone to read. But the best gift is that the Lord has taken great care to make sure we have Jacob's story to teach and encourage us when we have difficult times in our homes. Most families can easily identify with the story of Jacob and the situations his family encountered. So much can be learned from this family who could be the cast of the next, nighttime, television drama series.

There are dozens of issues which are revealed in this sordid story that parents face everyday. However, let's narrow down the story just a bit. Like Jacob, we have daughters who want to hang out with the wrong crowd, sons who do not deal well with anger and deceit in their hearts, and, if the truth be known, we have a hard time addressing difficult family issues properly. Fortunately, the Lord has the answer.

It must have been difficult for Dinah to live in a family where two sisters, Leah and Rachel, constantly competed for the attention of her father. The unending tension and jealousy between her mother and her step-mother/aunt must have been difficult to bear. It was a never-ending rivalry. A cloud always seemed to be hanging over their tents and no one could escape from the conflict. Had Dinah had all she could stand? Was the struggle too great? Was she wanting to escape the daily drama of her family? If so, she did it without parental approval. Or was she lonely? She was the lone female in a house full of boys. You would think that, being the only daughter in the family, Dinah would have had some special attention. The only girl in the middle of eleven brothers should have warranted some preferential treatment and given her reason to not leave the safety of her own home. Her reasons and motives for her excursion are unclear, but one thing is evident. Dinah's decision to leave the protection of her home resulted in tragedy.

At the outset of the story we find Dinah taking an ill-advised trip to visit pagan women of Canaan. Since the Bible does not give us any explanation for her actions, we have to take a closer look at the overall context of the narrative. Consider the town Jacob and his family lived near. Shechem was not Bethel. Bethel was where Jacob began his journey twenty plus years ago, and it was where he had promised to return. After his dream at Bethel, where he saw the angels of God ascending and descending on a stairway, he vowed to the Lord that he would come back and worship Him there. For some reason Jacob had delayed his return which resulted in disaster for his family. He was nineteen miles off course. What if Jacob had not postponed his arrival to Bethel? Many times we find ourselves with big problems when we are not where the Lord wants us to be. Jacob had his family in the wrong place at the wrong time. This does not excuse Dinah for her wandering, but it does teach us that when we delay on what God has called us to, especially as parents, bad things can happen.

Our dynamic duo, on the other hand, must have presented a completely different set of challenges for Jacob. Could it have been "deja vu all over again?" Imagine Jacob sitting at the entrance to his tent watching as a caravan of flocks, herds, donkeys, women, and children slowly approach him. As the convoy gets closer he notices wagons and carts full of produce from gardens and household items piled as high as each carriage could haul. He also sees his rescued daughter with her head hanging down in shame mixed in with the crowd. Leading the processional are his two sons who, at their last visit, seemed to be the ambassadors of peace between the two tribes. As the train makes its way up to his front door and comes to a stop what must have been going through the patriarch's mind? I cannot help but believe that as he gazed into his boys' eyes Jacob saw shades of his brother and himself in Simeon and Levi. Jacob knew without even asking what had taken place in Shechem. Shechem was no more! Standing before him were two boys filled with hate and deceit. As he looked into their faces, Jacob must have had flashbacks of a time he'd tried to forget. He saw in their countenance the same intense anger his brother Esau had toward him after he had tricked their father Isaac into giving him the family blessing. Even though Jacob and his brother had reconciled, these two boys reminded him of Esau. With everyone standing in silence, Jacob replayed in his mind the event that took place in his tent just a few short days ago. He remembered the excitement of two people groups becoming one family as Hamor and Shechem were asking for Dinah's hand in marriage. But the sad reality was that Simeon and Levi had all along been planning a massacre. Deception, his former way of life, was now in their blood.

Jacob's next words almost seem to come out of nowhere. He said nothing of their hate. He made no mention of their deceit, but took his conversation in a totally different direction. There was nothing wrong with what Jacob said to his sons. The overall safety of his family was extremely important. Maybe it wasn't what he said that leaves the story unsettled for us. Perhaps it was what he didn't say. He said and did nothing to address Dinah's, Simeon's or Levi's personal issues. Jacob was avoiding the problem and sticking his head in the sand.

LET'S GET PRACTICAL
Pastor Mark Holmen

Wow! Is your head spinning? There is a lot to get your mind wrapped around in this story. Have you had to read and reread portions of what Dr. Smith has written? If so, that's okay. We need to have our brains challenged, and when you go through the Old Testament you will encounter things that will challenge our abilities to see the forest (the big picture) because of the trees. So let me try to focus our attention on a couple of things.

First, families are messy, and the more you know about them the messier things get. If you were to dig into my family's history, you would encounter depression, anxiety, alcoholism, child endangerment, personal traumatic stress disorder, anger issues, cancer, and a whole host of other afflictions. So the first thing we need to understand is that families have issues and Jacob's family was no different. There is no such thing as a perfect family because all families are dysfunctional. Therefore, the question becomes: how as dysfunctional families do we become functional? In other words, how do we learn from dysfunctional family experiences? Whether they be from the families we grew up in or the families of others that we read about, how can we avoid making the same mistakes and repeating the same behaviors? I don't know about you but I want my family to be the very best it can be, so I am willing to spend time reading about and listening to stories about how other families handled their messy business because that helps me know how to better handle my own messy, family business.

The second thing I see in this story cannot be emphasized enough.

Honest communication is critical. Unfortunately, in any written account of a messy, family situation information is left out. But there is one thing I can see throughout this story of Jacob and his family that's not hard to pick out. They did not communicate as openly and honestly as they could have. Poor communication led them to make poor decisions that could have been avoided if they would have simply communicated better as a family.

As I work with families today, I would probably say that the number one issue families face is poor communication and that comes at a time when we have more ways to communicate than ever before. We can correspond through texting, cell phones, Facebook, Pinterest, Skype, e-mail, etc. Unfortunately, like we see in the story of Jacob, much of our communication today as families is shortened to quick, sound bites. We settle for using one hundred and twenty character tweets, or less, rather than taking the time to slow down and truly talk and listen so we can fully understand what is going on. Clearly Dinah did not feel she could talk openly and honestly to her father Jacob about what was going on in her life and why she wanted to venture out from her home. Clearly Jacob did not have open and honest conversation with Simeon and Levi about how they would handle the Shechemites. And clearly, no one truly addressed, through open communication, the hurt and pain caused to Dinah and the entire family as a result of her being raped. To be functional in a dysfunctional family, open communication is critical.

I would argue that the majority of family issues past, present, and future are the result of poor communication. We need to take the time to slow down, sit down, and truly talk to one another about what is really going on. As parents we must set the example and create safe environments so that open, honest communication can occur. So that these opportunities can take place, we may need to pull the van off to the side of the road or walk into a bedroom and shut the door. It could mean something as simple as going for a walk or visiting a park. You could also create a once a week ritual where you go on some sort of "date" or commit to having Sunday lunch together as a family. Bottom line, we need be intentional and take whatever steps necessary to allow open communication to flow naturally in our homes.

I can only imagine how things would have turned out differently for Jacob, Dinah, and their family if they had an environment where they could have talked openly and honestly together. Dinah could have had a daddy-daughter date night where she could have had an opportunity to talk openly and honestly with her dad about the unique struggles she faced as a girl. Maybe while helping with meal preparations in the kitchen, Leah could have made sure there was a comfortable atmosphere for a young girl to ask questions about friend choices and boys. Simeon and Levi could have talked openly and honestly with their dad over a Sunday dinner about their plans for the Shechemites. Then Jacob could have shared with them how revenge was not the answer. Do you see how open communication as a family could have changed so many things? Maybe Dinah never would have gone exploring. Maybe the rape never would have occurred. Maybe the destruction of the Shechemites never would have happened or maybe the family reputation would not have been destroyed.

So in closing this chapter I think we need to recognize that being a family is a messy business. It always has been and always will be.

No family is perfect, and all families will be dysfunctional. Yet we can learn from our dysfunctions, and we can get better. That is good news because we want to be the very best families we can be. So as we pull back to view the forest through the trees in this story, we realize that creating an environment where open and honest communication can occur is critical for families today. Failure to do so will lead to difficulties and mistakes that could easily be avoided by simply making the effort to create the opportunities for honest communication to occur. So let's make open and honest communication our first priority as we seek to become functional in our dysfunctional families.

LET'S TALK

Here are some questions I would like you to ponder and/or discuss:

1. Like Jacob, has the Lord called you to go to "Bethel" but you're still living in "Shechem"?

2. Do you know any older godly couples who have children that are older than yours? If so, try to connect with them and ask how they handled and dealt with messy situations in their families.

3. Ask your children, "How can I become a better listener?"

4. What "lines of communication" do you currently have for open and honest dialog with your children?

5. What new lines of communication do you intend on opening?

COURSE CORRECTION
Dr. Mark Smith

Hearing the phrase "Shechem is no more" is a hard pill to swallow. It's unimaginable to think that in only a few short days, two men were able to double-cross a ruler, betray all the men of a city, and bring total devastation to the small town just north of Bethel. All the buildings remained, but the people were gone. As a result of the massive slaughter, every man was dead. A once thriving city was now decimated- leaving the women without husbands and their children fatherless. All the survivors, possessions, and property were confiscated and relocated to a small settlement on the outskirts of town known as the house of Jacob.

Let's go back to the end of the previous chapter where Jacob was having a conversation with two of his sons. News of the bloodbath spread throughout the local communities, and Jacob was gripped with fear. He was consumed with the possibility of retaliation from neighboring tribes and convinced that the nearby residents would join together to kill him and his family because of the brutal assault by his two sons. With legitimate concern, Jacob had some very strong words to say to Simeon and Levi. From his human perspective, he thought he had good reason for sweating bullets and fearing the worst. He felt that revenge was inevitable. Although the situation seemed bleak, there was one very important thing Jacob failed to remember. God is the God of His word. With the threat of revenge looming in the air there were promises still in play.

The panic-stricken patriarch's back was pinned firmly against the wall, and he had nowhere left to turn. Talk about needing a Word from the Lord! But Jacob had not heard the Lord speak to him for a considerably long time. Then, out of nowhere, the loving voice of God said to Jacob, "Go up to Bethel and settle there, and build an altar there to God, who appeared to you when you were fleeing from your brother Esau" (Genesis 35:1). This was perfect timing. In that quiet and calming moment it is possible that the Lord's words jarred Jacob's mind back to his past. A decade before, while still living with Laban, the Lord came to Jacob and said, "I am the God of Bethel, where you anointed a pillar and where you made a vow to me. Now leave this land at once and go back to your native land" (Genesis 31:13). While the memory of these words played and replayed in his mind, Jacob knew deep in his heart exactly what the "God of Bethel" meant. "Go up to Bethel" was specific. The Lord didn't just want him back in his native land but wanted him to return to their special place...the place of promises. Bethel wasn't just a geographical location on a map; it was also the place where Jacob first met God thirty years before. Prior to all his wives, children, and wealth in Haran, Bethel was where God had made His promise to Jacob, the same ovenant promise He had made to his father Isaac and grandfather Abraham. But that's not all. As God was subtly reminding Jacob of His desire, Jacob remembered a second promise that was made. Bethel was also the place where Jacob had made a promise to God. The Bible says, "Jacob made a vow, saying, 'If God will be with me and will watch over me on this journey I am taking and will give me food to eat and clothes to wear so that I return safely to my father's household, then the Lord will be my God and this stone that I have set up as a pillar will be God's house, and of all that you give me I will give you a tenth'" (Genesis 28:20-22). As these words and memories began to penetrate and sear his heart, Jacob was ignited with a new zeal. Jacob, now more interested in listening to the voice of God instead of continuing to hear the words of his two murderous sons, was ready for a change of scenery and, most importantly, he was ready to make a transformation of his ways. At last, Jacob was receiving God's message loudly and clearly.

Before he would start preparing his family to make another long trek, Jacob first had to do some housekeeping. The Bible says, "So Jacob said to his household and to all who were with him, 'Get rid of the foreign gods you have with you, and purify yourselves and change your clothes. Then come, let us go up to Bethel, where I will build an altar to God, who answered me in the day of my distress and who has been with me wherever I have gone'"(Genesis 35:2-3). In the face of popular opinion, Jacob made a stand. Local culture and borrowed customs had dictated his family's actions for far too long. The people in his household had worshipped and been enslaved by their "little g" gods, but that situation was about to be corrected. Without hesitation he demanded radical changes from each wife, child, and servant before leaving Shechem. Jacob required everyone to cough up any and every type of trinket, figurine, or piece of jewelry that competed in their hearts with the One True God. So they did. Next he directed each person to ceremonially wash themselves. It wasn't just an act of scrubbing off the daily dirt and grime but a way to symbolically say to the Lord, "I'm removing the old to make ready for the new." They all obeyed. Finally, Jacob gave instructions for each servant and family member to put on new (or different) clothes. All complied. These acts would signify their willingness to submit to Jacob and his authority. More importantly it displayed their desire to commit themselves to the Lord.

The Bible says, "So they gave Jacob all the foreign gods they had and the rings in their ears, and Jacob buried them under the oak at Shechem" (Genesis 35:4). Jacob knew that he and his household would have to thoroughly purify themselves inwardly and totally elim-inate all idolatrous symbols outwardly before they could approach the holy God. For the first time in his life, the prodigal patriarch was stepping up and being the leader of his family, a position that had been lacking for a very long time. Based on his family's submission, it was apparently a welcomed change within the home.

However, there still remained the problem of the restless neighboring natives wanting to flex their retaliatory muscles. While Jacob was busy making arrangements to get out of Dodge, God was not sitting around twiddling His thumbs. He was, as He always is, moving to fulfill His great purpose. The Lord was working where no one could see to prepare the way for Jacob to make good on his promise. Ja-cob was doing all he could do as he prepared his family for depar-ture. However, God was about to do something that only He could do. The Bible says, "Then they set out, and the terror of God fell on the towns all around them so that no one pursued them" (Genesis 35:5). What was that terror? Was it a darkness, an audible sound or voice, confusion in the minds of the town's people and leaders? One thing is certain, whatever it was, it was the miraculous hand of a powerful God at work. In the end the Lord had Jacob where He wanted him. Jacob was back to where the story began.

Imagine the homecoming. As Jacob and his family arrived in Bethel the Bible says, "There he built an altar, and he called the place El Bethel, because it was there that God revealed himself to him when he was fleeing from his brother" (Genesis 35:7). Is it possible that as he was building the altar Jacob was genuinely worshipping the Lord and sincerely thanking Him for His faithfulness for the first time in his life? I can't help but believe that Jacob was praising God as he laid each stone on top of another. As he positioned each rock he could have said, "Thank you for being with me. You are truly Jehovah-Shammah (The Lord is There) because you never abandoned me. Lord, You are worthy of worship because You kept your promise by watching over me while I was away." As Jacob sacrificed a tenth of his livestock he must have said, "I exalt You because You proved Yourself to me as Jehovah-Jireh (The Lord will Provide) by giving me food to eat and clothes to wear. I praise You Lord for returning me home safely." Because God was the ultimate promise keeper, Jacob was now able to worship Him as a promise keeper himself. But we have to ask, "Where was his family?" The Bible says, "Jacob and all the people with him came to Luz (that is, Bethel) in the land of Canaan" (Genesis 35:6). Nothing suggests that his family was anywhere other than with Jacob during the entire time of worship. After arriving together in Bethel, the narrative has the patriarch busy building an altar there with his family. We find Jacob worshipping and leading his family in worship. Besides, they were all cleaned up, dressed up, and ready for church; where else would they be?

Before we leave this awesome scene in the lives of Jacob and his family, we need to stop and consider one important aspect of this episode. What was God's response during this whole ordeal? Was He pleased with Jacob's obedience and worship? Yes, was He ever! As a matter of fact, the Lord showed up in person to tell him so. The Bible says, "God appeared to him again and blessed him. The Lord said to him, 'Your name is Jacob, but you will no longer be called Jacob; your name will be Israel.' So he named him Israel" (Genesis

35:9b-10). This was much more than God reminding Jacob of the time He changed his name; He was redefining the course of his life. With His personal stamp of approval, 'Jacob' the 'heel grabber' or 'deceiver,' like Shechem, was no more. Until this point Jacob was only capable of being a reformed deceiver who struggled with God. But now God was intervening in his life and establishing a new direction for him and his family. This was a new day. Jacob heard the voice of God and decided it was time to be obedient to Him. With Jacob now surrendered to the Lord, God would no longer address him as 'heel grabber' or 'one who wrestles with God' but as 'the Prince of God.'

This was a defining moment in his life and a turning point for his family. But that was only a small part of God's blessing. Not only was God breathing new life into an old man and a dozen children, He was setting the course of an entire nation to come. The Bible says, "I am God Almighty; (El Shaddai) be fruitful and increase in number. A nation and a community of nations will come from you, and kings will be among your descendants. The land I gave to Abraham and Isaac I also give to you, and I will give this land to your descendants after you" (Genesis 35:11-12). This must have been music to Jacob's old, tired ears. Knowing that not only his immediate family would prosper in the new land but his future descendants would include royalty put a new fire in his aged bones and Jacob's first response was to worship. Scripture says, "Jacob set up a stone pillar at the place where God had talked with him, and he poured out a drink offering on it; he also poured oil on it. Jacob called the place where God had talked with him Bethel" (Genesis 35:13-15). Jacob was now a changed man. From this point forward, his sordid past would be a distant memory. Jacob underwent a transformation that could only be accomplished by a relentless, compassionate, and patient God known as El Shaddai (God Almighty).

To say Jacob was a stranger to the word "obedience" is an understatement. The idea of surrendering to God's desires was not a natural thing for him to do. In his case Jacob's problem was two-fold. He was prone to selfishness plus he had a streak of stubbornness. This combination inevitably pulled him deeper into rebellion and ultimately kept him at a distance from God. However, the Lord eventually won over Jacob's heart, but it came at a great cost. Many people lost their lives. In Jacob's case it took a crisis (a wakeup call) before God had his attention, but God did what God had to do.

If we are honest with ourselves, we are not that much different from Jacob. The reason we identify so easily with this old Biblical character is there is a little bit of a 'heel grabber' in all of us. If we are not careful, we too can fall prey to similar issues with relative ease. We can make so much of what we want and be so inwardly focused that everything and everyone else gets left on the sidelines. To that end, there are several questions we should and must ask ourselves. "Are there things in my own life, or in my home, with which I need to deal with before I can truly worship?" "Am I properly leading my family in worship of the Almighty God?" "Will God have to bring a crisis into my life, or the life of my family, before I wake up?" We need to wrestle with these questions. However, there is another, more-pressing question to consider: "What's my reaction time?" In other words, "What is the amount of time between God's action and my reaction to what He desires? How sensitive am I to His voice?"

When we don't have selfishness, stubbornness, etc... in the way, our reaction time is often pretty quick. However, when we seem to delay or even ignore God's activity in our lives there is a reason. For a follower of Jesus Christ delay is most certainly always sin. After leaving Laban's house, Jacob struggled with his reaction time. It took ten years and a crisis before he decided it was time to be obedient to the Lord. But his second opportunity was entirely different. There was little to no delay in Jacob's reaction to God's voice. Within seconds, as his family stood by his side, he was standing up a rock, uncorking bottles of wine and oil, and pouring them out as a drink offering to the Lord. Therefore, we have to ask ourselves, "What is our reaction time when God speaks?" Remember, you have a family who needs an example.

LET'S GET PRACTICAL
Pastor Mark Holmen

I don't know about you, but I find myself falling in and out of love with God. Perhaps it is better to say I find my love for God sliding back and forth (on a scale of 1-10) between 4 and 8 a lot. I also know the Bible says we are to love the Lord with ALL our heart, soul and strength. While that is something I deeply desire to do, it's amazing how I can still find myself sliding up and down the "love scale" in my relationship with God. And since I'm being honest, I might as well go all the way and say that this same love "sliding" also happens in my relationship with my wife. While I would like to see my love for her always remain at a ten, that simply isn't the case. But there is one thing I have learned. Every time I feel my love for her sliding downward on the scale, all I need to do is to go on a date with her or go out for pizza together, and my love slide starts moving back up the scale. Let me explain.

When I first met Maria she was in another relationship so I waited patiently for her to dump the guy, recognizing that there was a better option. Then I moved in and asked if she wanted to go on a date. She agreed. So I picked her up one evening and off we went to Pizza Hut. (As I was a poor college student, this was about as good as I could do at that time.) When we sat down, I asked her what kind of pizza she would like. She said, "pepperoni" which was a good sign because that was my favorite kind of pizza as well. Normally when I order a pepperoni pizza by myself I put salt on it, but I also know that girls think that is gross. I knew better than to do that on a date. When the pizza arrived, we were in the middle of a great conversation. I served her a piece of pizza and put one on my plate as well.

Because I was not paying attention, I instinctively reached for the salt shaker and began putting salt on my piece. Then I realized what I was doing, and not wanting to destroy what seemed to be a good start, I tried to slyly put the salt shaker away without her noticing. Just when I thought I had completed the deception successfully, she looked at me and said, "Are you done with the salt, and if so, could you pass it to me?" Then she proceeded to put salt on her piece of pizza. At that moment I knew she was the one! Now, as silly as it seems, whenever I need to increase my love for Maria all I need to do is take her for pizza and watch her put salt on her pieces. I fall back in love all over again.

Friends, as we have discussed previously, the best thing we can do to help our kids love Christ is to show them that we love Christ. If our love for Christ does not seem as strong as it should, maybe we should go back and remember who Christ is and what He has done for us. It doesn't surprise me that when God wanted to reestablish Jacob, He took him back to the place that would serve to stir up his love for God all over again. I have certain places and things that remind me who God is and draw me closer to Him. For example, when I'm on the boat listening to worship music, I am reminded of so many things God has done for me. Another place where my heart is stirred is at a Christian concert or some worship event where the music is played loudly and everyone is just singing out praises to God.

So I guess I have a simple question for you. Where is your Bethel? Where is your place where you connect with God best? Where do you reestablish your relationship with Him? Where do you go to increase your love when it has slid a little? And here's the most critical question: are you getting there often enough? If you're married, talk to your spouse about this and make sure you are supporting each other's ability to get to your personal Bethel. And if you have children, start to engage them in this process as well. Make sure you are giving them time and opportunities to get to their Bethel. If we don't do this, we will begin to slowly forget God or lose some of our love for Him like when you take a log out of the fire and it slowly begins to lose its flame, redness, and heat.

LET'S TALK

Here are some questions I would like you to ponder and/or discuss:

1. Share the little and big things that God has done for you that make you love Him.

2. As you think of a 1-10 love scale, where would you say your love for Christ is at this moment? Do you find it changing, and if so, what drives that change?

3. Where are your "Bethels" that help you increase your love for Christ?

4. Are you getting to your Bethels enough? If not, why not?

5. What do you need in order to make sure you are able to get to your Bethels?

BLATANT PARTISANSHIP
Dr. Mark Smith

Having favorites is a fun part of life. For instance, you can have a favorite television show, style of food, music genre, or sports team. When you have favorites, it naturally means you have other things that are not your favorites. You can have television shows, food, music, and teams for which you do not care. There is no harm in showing partiality in this way because the Lord has made us all different; we all have unique and diverse interests. On the other hand, it's quite another matter to allow yourself to show favoritism toward people. When a person is given preferential treatment, it has the potential of making everybody else feel less important. To compound the problem even further, when a parent shows favoritism toward anyone in the home, it can cause devastating division and hurt in the family.

In all the Bible it's hard to find a better character to show us the negative effects favoritism can cause in the home than Jacob. He showed favoritism to not one but two family members. Jacob had a favorite wife and a favorite son which multiplied the problem considerably when he had three other wives and eleven other sons.

Favoritism was not a new concept in Jacob's world. From conception, Jacob and his twin brother Esau were rivals in and outside the womb. We first hear about his encounter with favoritism in his childhood because it was a disease to which his parents had exposed him early in life. Scripture tells us that, "the boys grew up, and Esau

79

became a skillful hunter, a man of the open country, while Jacob was content to stay at home among the tents. Isaac, who had a taste for wild game, loved Esau, but Rebekah loved Jacob" (Genesis 25:27-28). In other words, favoritism was firmly planted in his parents' household. Unfortunately, it was a way of life which Jacob would later carry into his own home.

As expected, when something as volatile as favoritism is present in people's lives, they can say and do some very hurtful things. Jacob's life was no exception. The Bible gives us some details about Jacob's life and how the effects of favoritism played out. Let's retrace our steps and retell the story in a bit more detail of the first part of Jacob's married life to see the rippling effects of favoritism.

When he was about seventy years old, Jacob was at a crossroads in his life. He was in Haran at the local watering hole catching his breath after being on the run from his angry sibling. Esau was on a mission to kill his brother. Jacob had stolen the family blessing his father had intended to give his twin, so Jacob hit the road. As Jacob was getting his bearings, the most stunning woman he had ever seen walked right into his life. Like every other day, Rachel was busy going through her regular routine of chores. One of her responsibilities was to make sure her father's livestock had their daily ration of water. As Rachel approached the well, she caught Jacob's eye. Was it love at first sight? We're not told, but one thing was certain; Jacob was captivated and he knew he would have to talk to her daddy before he could make any moves. Fortunately for our eligible bachelor her father just so happened to be his uncle. Within a month's time, Jacob had made up his mind and decided he would do whatever was necessary to have Rachel as his bride. The Bible says, "Jacob was in love with Rachel and said, 'I'll work for you seven years in return for your younger daughter Rachel.' Laban said, 'It's better that I give her to you than to some other man. Stay here with me.' So Jacob served seven years to get Rachel, but they seemed like only a few days to him because of his love for her" (Genesis 29:18-20). For most people seven years is a long time...but not when you're in love.

Jacob worked seven years to earn the hand of the beautiful Rachel, and finally the day arrived. However, little did Jacob know that his uncle Laban had pulled the wool over his eyes by doing the old 'switch the bride in the dress' trick. When he woke up the next morning, Jacob found himself beside a woman he wasn't expecting. According to their customs, Laban's oldest daughter Leah had to be the first to get married, not her younger sister Rachel. If he was going to get anywhere with his father in-law, Jacob was going to have to strike a new deal to have any chance at marrying the bride of his dreams. After the marriage week was complete with Leah, Jacob got the green light to fulfill his desires with Rachel. Two weddings in a matter of days would come with a hefty price tag. The Bible says, "Jacob made love to Rachel also, and his love for Rachel was greater than his love for Leah. And he worked for Laban another seven years" (Genesis 29:30). The price was not the extended work release program negotiated with Uncle Laban but the virus of favoritism Jacob would carry into his new family. Within days, the new groom had unintentionally started a war between his brides.

There was no love lost between Leah and Rachel. As a result of Jacob's favoritism the sisters were in a constant battle with one other. For Leah, she longed for more than only meeting her husband's sexual desires. She yearned for a loving husband, dedicated companion, and a lifelong soulmate. Leah never seemed to receive from Jacob what she hungered for the most. Jacob only gave his affections to Rachel. His attention was something she never lacked. Even though Rachel had his love and full devotion, the Lord had compassion on Leah and blessed her with fertility. As you recall, when Leah had her first child, she pridefully called him Reuben which means 'look a son.' This can easily be seen as an attempt on Leah's part to turn Jacob's heart toward herself. Who can blame her? She did give him a son. However, this can also be viewed as a relentless mental and verbal jab. In other words, Leah wanted to rub her sister's face in the fact that she was first to give Jacob a son.

To make things more difficult, after Leah had her fourth son Levi, Rachel's frustration with her infertility was at it's peak. In desperation she decided to give Jacob her maidservant, Bilhah, to be her surrogate. Rachel said, "Here is Bilhah, my servant. Sleep with her so that she can bear children for me and I too can build a family through her" (Genesis 30:3). Bilhah did conceive on two different occasions. Oddly enough, Leah had stopped having children which only meant one thing...the contest was going to a new level. It didn't take long before Leah made Jacob the same offer with her maidservant, Zilpah, and she too gave birth to two boys.

Favoritism in Jacob's life was not just limited to his wives. This sickness went well beyond them into his relationships with his sons. Scripture tells us, "Now Israel loved Joseph more than any of his other sons, because he had been born to him in his old age..." (Genesis 37:3a). It is evident that Jacob had a nasty recurring theme in his close relationships. It's one thing for Jacob to have loved Rachel more than Leah; however, it is quite another for him to have loved Joseph more than his other sons. Aside from the fact that showing favoritism can cause numerous problems in relationships, Jacob should have considered the ten other guys to whom he was showing less love. This was not just any random crew; these were vicious and unscrupulous men who were unconcerned with consequences pertaining to their actions. When mistreated, these sons of Jacob could be merciless even to their own kin. The Bible tells us that, "...and he (Jacob) made an ornate robe for him (Joseph). When his brothers saw that their father loved him more than any of them, they hated him and could not speak a kind word to him" (Genesis 37:3b-4).

Jacob's predisposition for 'greater than' and 'more than' with his love always spelled disaster. Joseph, a seventeen year old boy who was doted on by his father, had just received a tailor-made suit from his dad. However, this was not just any fashion statement. When Jacob adorned his son with this robe, he was telling his entire family that not only was Joseph his favorite but also that he would be the next leader of all the sons. With an already rocky sibling rivalry firmly in place, Jacob, with one article of clothing, put the nail in Joseph's coffin. As expected, the fancy coat did not go over well with the brothers. In the end, their hate would escalate into a murderous plot to eliminate their little brother.

The brothers knew that confronting Jacob's favoritism was a hopeless cause. Instead, they came up with an evil plan to permanently rid themselves of their robed irritant. As the brothers convened they said to one another, "Come now, let's kill him and throw him into one of these cisterns and say that a ferocious animal devoured him. Then we'll see what comes of his dreams" (Genesis 37:20). Reuben, who was probably ranked dead last on Jacob's favorite-people list, came to Joseph's rescue by convincing his brothers that murder was not the answer. With all the brothers agreeing to this new direction, they ripped off his robe and dropped him in a deep hole to rot. Knowing that Joseph would soon be dead, all the brothers except Reuben sat down and enjoyed a meal together. Then (entering stage left) the Lord sends a caravan of Ishmaelites heading to Egypt to sell their merchandise. With Reuben out running errands, Judah became the voice of reason saying, "'What will we gain if we kill our brother and cover up his blood? Come, let's sell him to the Ishmaelites and not lay our hands on him; after all, he is our brother, our own flesh and blood.' His brothers agreed" (Genesis 37:26-27) and Joseph had a one way ticket to Egypt.

As the dust was settling with the caravan disappearing slowly out of sight Reuben, Simeon, Levi, Judah, Issachar, Zebulun, Dan, Naphtali, Gad and Asher must have thought all their troubles were over. With Joseph clearly out of the picture all that was left to do was take dad the evidence of a fatal struggle with a wild beast. "They took the ornate robe back to their father and said, 'We found this. Examine it to see whether it is your son's robe.' He recognized it and said, 'It is my son's robe! Some ferocious animal has devoured him. Joseph has surely been torn to pieces'" (Genesis 37:32-33). Without uttering a single word, they allowed their father's imagination to run wild which resulted in breaking his heart.

LET'S GET PRACTICAL
Pastor Mark Holmen

Throughout this passage we are confronted with the damaging effects favoritism can have on the lives of individuals and families. I would love to say this type of favoritism doesn't exist today, but as a former youth and family pastor I encountered it repeatedly. I want to be clear that favoritism is not the same as having more in common with one child than another. It's normal and almost to be expected that children are going to have some things in common with one parent more than with the other. It is also not unusual to see that as your child grows, he will go back and forth from being a "momma's boy" to a "daddy's boy." Through the years we have definitely gone through "seasons" where my daughter has been closer to her mom and seasons where she is closer to me. That's not favoritism because favoritism is the practice of giving unfair preferential treatment to one person or group at the expense of another. So with favoritism there are two sins being committed: first you are giving "unfair" treatment to one person and secondly you are doing this at the "expense" of another.

Have you ever been treated unfairly? I think we all have and can recall a situation where we encountered unfair treatment. How did that make you feel? Were you treated unfairly as a child, or did you have friends who were treated unfairly in their home environments? What was that like for you or them? I don't know about you, but when I am treated unfairly I instantly become angry and aggressive because I'm upset with the way I'm being treated. And I want people to know that what's happening to me is unfair.

Recently my daughter and I were on the hunt for two paddle boards, and we called Costco. I spoke with a salesperson and was told that they had two in stock. Instantly I told the person to whom I was talking that we wanted both of them. I asked if they could put them on hold until we got there. She informed me that Costco has a "no holds" policy so everything is sold on a "first come" basis. My daughter and I hopped in the truck and headed right over to the store arriving there in twenty minutes. We walked in and an employee asked if we needed help to which I responded, "Yes, we are here to get paddle boards. We just called in and were told you had two left so we would like to get both of them please." The employee responded, "I'm sorry but we only have one left to sell because the other paddle board in on hold for someone." Now I was upset. After my mini tirade, the employee went on to explain that after our phone call a woman had come in looking for a paddle board but she didn't have a truck so they put one of the paddle boards on hold until she could go and get a truck from a friend. That explanation clearly did not make things better, but I could see that blowing up at the salesperson any further was not going to get me anywhere so I simply asked to talk to the store manager. When the manager arrived, I explained to him that we had called looking for two paddle boards and when we were told they only had two left, we tried to put the them on hold but were told we couldn't. But much to our surprise, when we arrived, we were told that one of the paddle boards was put on hold after our phone call so now we could only get one. But we wanted two. I told him it was "unfair" that someone else could put a paddle board on hold when we were told that could not be done. I simply asked the manger to honor his "no holds" policy, and he left saying, "I'm going to go see what happened." A few minutes later he came back with both paddle boards on a cart and said, "You are right, we have a no holds policy so since you are here you can have both paddle boards." My daughter and I were thrilled so we purchased both paddle boards, loaded them in the truck, and got out of there as fast as possible before the woman came back looking for her paddle board!

This story illustrates, in a short manner, what happens when we are treated unfairly. We get upset, angry, and defensive. It drives us to want to right the wrong doing whatever it takes to get that done. I must confess that many times the way I act or respond to unfair treatment is sometimes as unchristian or sin-filled as the unfair treatment itself. I can get so upset with unfair treatment that it can lead me to say terrible things and act like a total jerk. For some reason, I feel justified in doing this simply because I have been treated unfairly. So my point is the fact that not only do I not like what unfair treatment does to me, I also detest what it brings out of me because many times it causes me to say and do things I would normally never say or do to people.

In the same way, I feel favoritism in families is damaging in two ways. It is not only hurtful to the ones who are the victims of unfair treatment, but it also drives them to act, say, and do things they would normally never do. And then parents, not recognizing that they are treating one or more of their children unfairly, get more upset at the victimized children for their aggressive behavior, and it becomes a vicious circle. Just think about it. If one instance of unfair treatment, like what happened to me at Costco, can get me upset and flying off the handle, imagine what happens in households where there is constant favoritism. It creates a volatile and toxic environment to say the least.

So now what? The point of this chapter is to confront one major thing in families, and that is favoritism. God shows no favoritism toward us; therefore, we are called to show no favoritism toward one another and that should especially be true in the way our children are raised today.

LET'S TALK

Here are some questions I would like you to ponder and/or discuss:

1. Based on this chapter, how would you now define favoritism?

2. Have you experienced the hurt of favoritism in your past?

3. Is there favoritism in your home?

4. Are there animosities or tensions in your home because of your partiality toward another person?

5. If so, what are you going to do to change it? (There is no room for favoritism in Christ-centered families).

DUPLICATING PROCESS

Dr. Mark Smith

Mission Accomplished! Operation "Nemesis Deportation" was a complete success. As they left their distraught father holding his favorite son's ravaged coat of many colors and bloodstains, the sons of Jacob were ready to celebrate. Oh sure, they saw how crushed their father was at the thought of never seeing Joseph again, but that didn't matter. To them, their father's pain was only a minor side effect. In their minds they were justified. They were finally rid of their boastful, tattle-tale, ornamental-robe- strutting, little brother. These ten men could care less that their one lie would devastate their father for the next twenty years. All they were concerned about was that Joseph was permanently out of their hair...or so they thought.

Meanwhile, as Joseph was watching his homeland slowly disappear out of sight from the porthole of his traveling detention center, the Lord was preparing a rigorous training program for His servant. God would put Joseph through a series of improbable circumstances and precariously work in his life for the next several years to get him ready to save the world. The Bible tells us that Joseph was sold as a slave to an Egyptian leader known as Potiphar. He quickly rose to prominence in his house only later to fall out of favor because of an adulterous wife. As he was enduring a long stint in prison, the Lord sent him two palace employees as cellmates. While there, the cupbearer and the baker each had dreams about their future that they did not understand. God used Joseph to interpret their dreams with pinpoint accuracy. As they were released from prison, Joseph had hopes that his new best friend, the cupbearer, would remember him and send a "get out of jail free" card; but he did not. Sadly, with each passing day our jailbird only found himself re-wearing the same striped pajamas. Joseph could see no end in sight to his incarceration; however, the Lord had not forgotten him. Then, out of nowhere, God gave the Egyptian ruler a strange dream that only one man could decode. Before we know it, Pharaoh is shaking things up with his leadership and making Joseph his assistant in preparation for the famine of the century.

The new Egyptian second-in-command had a very busy first nine years in office. In his first seven years he brilliantly organized crop producers to supply enough grain to care for the normal needs of the nation plus have an abundant surplus. As the extra grain began to pile up, he had numerous storage facilities built to handle the overflow. Egypt's new business tycoon masterfully executed this plan for seven bountiful years until God turned off the switch. Just as the Lord had allowed seven years of plenty, Egypt was now bracing itself for seven years of nothing. It only took two short years before people outside of Egypt were in great need of food. Grain was in high demand and a precious commodity throughout the known world. Egypt was now in command of the market.

As expected, the famine took its toll on Jacob and his family's food supply. As the rainless months wore on, his family's grain reserves were depleted. Brought to a point of desperation, Jacob and his sons had only one place to turn...Egypt. Yet this was no ordinary famine; it had a much greater purpose. God had specifically designed and orchestrated this event to bring a family back together.

People from the entire region were coming to the world's most famous agricultural distributer to purchase enough grain to survive. No one, except Egypt, was prepared for this cataclysmic event and people were starving, especially in Canaan. Jacob realized it was time to light a fire under his sons' backsides and get them busy securing some grain for their family. He had seen on the Evening News (just kidding) that Egypt had grain, so he called his sons, minus Benjamin, together and said, "Why do you just keep looking at each other? I have heard that there is grain in Egypt. Go down there and buy some for us, so that we may live and not die" (Genesis 42:1-2). It didn't take long before the ten brothers saddled up and made their way to see the second most powerful man in the world. However, the governor of Egypt wasn't just another political figure in a distant land. He was certainly the man they wanted to meet, but the last guy they wanted to face.

The brothers finally made it to the Egyptian leader's courts and were given an opportunity to speak directly to the man himself. Little did they know that the man they were standing in front of was Joseph, the boy they sold as a slave to a bunch of nomads some two decades before. From this point forward the book of Genesis describes in detail how Joseph hid his identity from his brothers. As each chapter unfolds, we see the quiet desperation of Joseph wanting reconciliation with his brothers but instead holding himself back. In time, Joseph would reveal his true identity to his brothers but not until he had systematically proven to himself that they were ready for reconciliation.

Much like his father had been with Esau, Joseph was very deliberate with every word he spoke. In typical Jacob-like fashion, he carefully calculated each move he made in order to set his unsuspecting brothers up to determine the true condition of their hearts. He was a chip-off-the-old block. However, Joseph didn't stop there. He continued by putting pressure on his brothers by accusing them of being spies. In an attempt to prove their innocence, the terrified brothers gave a brief synopsis of their family history to try and convince their accuser otherwise. Joseph knew they were telling the truth but refused to let up with his masquerade. Just before the brothers were about to head for home, Joseph tightened the screws even more by keeping Simeon, one of their group of ten, as a hostage in exchange for their youngest brother Benjamin. Knowing this would not set well with dad, the brothers apprehensively made their way home. As they were departing Reuben concluded, "Didn't I tell you not to sin against the boy? But you wouldn't listen! Now we must give an accounting for his blood" (Genesis 42:22). This was the flicker of hope Joseph was wanting to hear. But were they ready for reconciliation?

The ten brothers had to go home now and face their aging father. When they told Jacob the news of what Egypt's governor wanted, the Patriarch hit the roof. There was no way he was going to allow his youngest and now most-favored son out of his sight, much less have him carried off to Egypt. But the grain eventually ran out, and now Jacob had a hard decision to make. He knew his sons could not show up in Egypt and receive grain without bringing Benjamin with them. He cried, "You have deprived me of my children. Joseph is no more and Simeon is no more, and now you want to take Benjamin. Everything is against me" (Genesis 42:36)! But Judah came out of nowhere to make one final petition to his father, a plea that described the true heart of his son. He swore to Jacob, "Send the boy along with me and we will go at once, so that we and you and our children

94

may live and not die. I myself will guarantee his safety; you can hold me personally responsible for him. If I do not bring him back to you and set him here before you, I will bear the blame before you all my life" (Genesis 43:8-9). Jacob knew he had no other choice but to let Benjamin go with his brothers, so they departed.

With the arrival of the Canaanite delegation back in Egypt, Joseph was still in disguise. Without revealing his true identity, the governor continued his interrogation of his brothers to see the genuineness of their hearts. Were they still self-centered or had they allowed the Lord to change them? Could he finally trust them and be reconciled to his brothers? This would be yet another test. Joseph immediately noticed the new kid in their group and sent his brothers to his home for lunch. When Joseph arrived, remaining in character, "they (the brothers joined by Simeon) presented to him the gifts they had brought into the house, and they bowed down before him to the ground" (Genesis 43:26). Joseph made small talk by asking about the health of their father while he gazed at all eleven brothers. When he saw Benjamin, his own mother's son, Joseph asked, "Is this your youngest brother, the one you told me about" (Genesis 43:29)? Overwhelmed with emotion, Joseph almost blew his cover but excused himself to regain his composure. Back in investigating mode, Joseph systematically arranged his brothers in order of their birth. From the oldest all the way down to the youngest they sat in chronological order, but it was hard not to notice the preferential treatment Benjamin received. Again Joseph was being strategic... just like dad.

Joseph prepared for his brothers' departure back to Canaan, but this time he sabotaged their return by placing his silver cup in Benjamin's sack of grain. Just as they got out of sight, Joseph sent one of his battalions after them. They had the brothers dismount and then inspected their sacks, of course, to find the planted, silver cup. Now the brothers were in dire straights because they had to go back and face the Egyptian leader...this time as presumed thieves.

Remaining undercover, Joseph put them to the final test. Would they rat out their youngest brother or rally around him? When all was said and done, the brothers pulled together and came to Benjamin's defense. What happened next was what Joseph had been building up to and longing for the whole time. Judah, speaking as the family ambassador, would sacrifice himself for his little brother. He said,"Please let your servant remain here as my lord's slave in place of the boy, and let the boy return with his brothers. How can I go back to my father if the boy is not with me? No! Do not let me see the misery that would come on my father" (Genesis 44:33-34). Judah had become Benjamin's redeemer.

With that final statement Joseph went from being a cloaked investigator to an emotional mess. Joseph could not keep up his pretense any longer. The Bible says, "Joseph could no longer control himself before all his attendants, and he cried out, 'Have everyone leave my presence!' So there was no one with Joseph when he made himself known to his brothers. And he wept so loudly that the Egyptians heard him, and Pharaoh's household heard about it" (Genesis 45:1-2). In other words, in total abandonment, he lost all composure and "he threw his arms around his brother Benjamin and wept, and Benjamin embraced him, weeping. And he kissed all his brothers and wept over them" (Genesis 45:14-15). In an instant, Joseph went from acting like his father Jacob to acting like his uncle Esau.

The old saying that the apple doesn't fall far from the tree certainly applies here. Joseph saw firsthand from his dad how to be methodical, systematic, and diplomatic when seeking to make things right. From Esau, he learned how to be totally abandoned and unrestrained when it comes to reconciliation. As a young boy, Joseph had a perfect view of what true forgiveness and reconciliation was all about and let it play out with his own brothers. Little did his father and uncle know that Joseph would someday emulate them in the art of reuniting. They taught him well.

LET'S GET PRACTICAL
Pastor Mark Holmen

What I love about this story is the way you get to see a family grow, change, evolve, function, and be dysfunctional. Every family is the same. If I were to tell the story of my family going back one hundred years, you would see a similar reality of a family that has grown, changed, evolved, functioned, and "dysfunctioned" over the course of those years. I'm sure the same can be said about your family. While each of our journeys are different, we are all on a journey nonetheless. Another thing that we all share in common with this Biblical family is the fact that God is at work in and through our family's journey whether we recognize it or not.

I would like to hit the pause button for a minute and simply ask you to reflect awhile on that last point. God is at work in and through our family's journey whether we recognize it or not. How does that make you feel? As you look back over the past one hundred years, can you see how God has been at work? Can you see how God's hand has been faithfully guiding and protecting you along the way? Can you see that even through the difficulties God has been at work? And even though your family journey has had ups and downs, roadblocks and potholes, turns and speed bumps, God has still kept you going as a family. God has never forsaken us even though we have had times when we have turned from him. God has not let us crash and burn even though we have done self-destructive things that could have destroyed us. God has been at work through our journey to bring us to the place we are today even when we were not working with Him. I don't know about you, but for me that reality definitely reminds me of how great our God is and how amazing his grace is. That truth simply makes me love and want to serve him all the more.

So I guess what I'm trying to help you do, in this portion of the book, is to acknowledge and see how God has been faithfully guiding, nudging, protecting and providing for your family so that you can recognize that God loves you and your family. He truly does! He loves you in spite of your family's flaws, mistakes, and missteps over the years. God doesn't care about those things although he would have loved to help you avoid them, but he desperately cares about you and your family. In fact, you matter so much to Him that He has given his one and only Son, Jesus Christ, so that you and your family's journey will continue on through death to eternity! God does not want death to be the end for you or anyone in your family. He has been faithfully guiding your family through the journey you have been on, because He has a plan and purpose for each of you. His purpose is for each of you to know, love, accept, and follow him through death to eternal life. God wants all of you to experience the full life you were created for where there will be no pain, suffering, hardship, famine, or disease. How does that sound?

Sometimes I think we make the Christian walk more difficult than it needs to be. For me it comes down to simply living in love with God which is pretty easy to do when you look back and see all the loving things God has done for us. How can I not love a God who has faithfully guided, protected, delivered and provided for me and my family even when I wasn't asking for or deserving of it? Yet one of the concerns I have for Christianity today is that we have a lot of people who are "doing" church but they are not "in love" with God. Often we have not taken the time to truly reflect on who God is and all the things He has done for us over the years.

With that said, what do you think is the number one reason why our children make the decision to be Christ-followers? The most important influence that leads children to faith in Christ is the faith of their parents. Essentially your kids are going to love who and what you love. So if you want your kids to love Christ, then the easiest way for that to happen is for you to love Christ and live a life that reflects you are in love with Him. Through the Biblical story we have been reading, we can get caught up in the actions and behaviors of the characters and lose sight of the main story line which is the unending and undeniable love of God who is faithfully guiding and leading each person through life. The hero of the story is not Jacob, Joseph, nor anyone else. It is God and his love for each of these people. That same God has that same love for you and your family. Don't ever lose sight of this truth.

LET'S TALK

Here are some questions I would like you to ponder and/or discuss:

1. How has God been at work in your family over the past one hundred years?

2. What were some ways that God lovingly guided your family to where you are today? (Some of them could have been tough love.)

3. How "in love" with God would you say you are on a scale of 1-10? Now, if you want a true litmus test, ask your children to rate your love for God and see if it is similar to where you rate yourself.

4. What are some specific things you do, or can do, to live a life that reflects that you are "in love" with God?

INTENTIONAL GROUNDING
Dr. Mark Smith

"Your father is ill" (Genesis 48:1) are some of the most unnerving and unsettling words a son could ever hear about his dad. There are countless other words or phrases we would rather have someone use when giving us the latest news about our father. For instance, we would want people to say, "Your father is awesome," "Your father is really a caring and loving man," or "Your father is a great and Godly man." But instead when the word 'ill' is placed in the blank there is a harsh reality tied to that thought, especially when your father is over one hundred and thirty years old.

Without hesitation, Joseph gathered his two sons, Manasseh and Ephraim, and headed over to his dad's house. Jacob received the news that his beloved son and grandsons were on their way to visit so he "rallied his strength and sat up on the bed" (Genesis 48:2). As the threesome entered the room, Jacob with delight began to reminisce. The feeble patriarch wasted no time in talking about his Lord. Jacob said, "God Almighty appeared to me at Luz in the land of Canaan, and there he blessed me and said to me, 'I am going to make you fruitful and increase your numbers. I will make you a community of peoples, and I will give this land as an everlasting possession to your descendants after you'" (Genesis 48:3-4). Chances are, Jacob never grew tired of telling others about this pivotal point in his life.

Joseph and his sons must have always enjoyed their visits with Jacob, but this time would be different. As Jacob was getting weaker with every passing day, he knew in his heart that for him to return again to the Promised Land would not be in God's plan. But he was confident that one day his family would multiply and occupy the land the Lord had promised. With wondrous thoughts and future visions of a blossoming family in a bountiful land, Jacob was content with passing on the family mantle to his sons. Before he would gather his entire family together to receive his departing blessing, the patriarch wanted to begin with Joseph. Jacob said to his son, "Now then, your two sons born to you in Egypt before I came to you here will be reckoned as mine; Ephraim and Manasseh will be mine, just as Reuben and Simeon are mine" (Genesis 48:5). Jacob was staking his claim on their lives. By taking Ephraim and Manasseh and making them his own, Jacob was elevating his grandsons to an equal status with Joseph and his brothers. Then Jacob said to his son, "Please bring them to me, and I will bless them" (Genesis 48:9b) and Joseph proudly did as his father requested.

This must have been a bittersweet moment for Joseph. Even though he knew that his aging father would not be with him much longer, he was given the precious opportunity of witnessing his sons receive an inheritance from his dad that had originated in the heart of God. The same promise Abraham received and passed down to his son Isaac who passed down to Jacob, Joseph was getting to take part in watching his sons, Ephraim and Manasseh, receive the great family blessing. As the boys pressed into their grandfather, Jacob embraced and kissed them. With respect and reverence of this great moment, Joseph bowed with his face to the floor. After a few minutes, Joseph raised and placed Ephraim, his youngest, on Jacob's left and positioned Manasseh, his oldest, to his father's right. Joseph was only doing what he thought to be the customary thing to do in the arrangement of his sons. He assumed his oldest would receive the greater blessing. "Then Israel stretched out his right hand and laid it on Ephraim's head, who was the younger, and his left hand on Manasseh's head, guiding his hands knowingly, for Manasseh was the firstborn. Then he blessed Joseph and said, 'May the God before whom my fathers Abraham and Isaac walked faithfully, the God who has been my shepherd all my life to this day, the Angel who has delivered me from all harm—may he bless these boys. May they be called by my name and the names of my fathers Abraham and Isaac, and may they increase greatly on the earth'" (Genesis 48:14-16).

As this auspicious occasion unfolded, Joseph was surprised to see what he thought was a mistake by his father. He noticed that his father's hands were crossed and resting on the wrong heads (his right hand on the younger and his left on the older) signifying the greater blessing going to Ephraim. In the heat of the moment he took his father's hand and tried to correct the situation and said to him, "Not so, my father, for this one is the firstborn; put your right hand on his head" (Genesis 48:18). But to Joseph's astonishment his father was fully aware of his words and actions. Jacob reassured his son when he said, "I know, my son, I know. He also shall become a people, and he also shall be great; but truly his younger brother shall be greater than he, and his descendants shall become a multitude of nations" (Genesis 48:19).

As we can see, Jacob purposefully and deliberately blessed the younger over the older. A move like this seems strange and untraditional; however, we have to remember this is the family line of Abraham. There is nothing ordinary or traditional about these people. Being the younger brother and being chosen over the oldest son is actually the norm for this clan. Isaac was the second son who was chosen over Ismael; Jacob was the second son who was chosen over Esau; and now we have Ephraim, the youngest, being chosen over his older brother Manasseh. As strange as this cycle seems, it was actually God's design.

This family reunion between Jacob, his son, and two grandsons was a beautiful picture of the patriarch adopting Joseph's sons as his own and passing down God's blessing to his children. All-in-all there doesn't appear to be a great deal in this story too farfetched when you consider whose family it is. From our perspective the scene is a picturesque ending to Jacob's otherwise crazy life. The whole passing of the torch was a great way to bring his chaotic life to a climatic close and a well-deserved peaceful decrescendo. We can assume that Joseph and both boys tell Jacob goodbye, hop into their chariot, and head back home just in time for dinner. The curtain is just about to close, the credits are ready to scroll up the screen, and we are anxiously hoping that the producers are going to end the movie by showing us some outtakes and bloopers of Jacob's life. All appears normal as the scene quietly closes out Genesis 48 with God's abundant grace intertwined throughout the entire get-together. What a good ending....almost too good.

When we look deeper into the story, we have to admit that it closes a bit too clean. How did this scene end so well? When we compare this ending to the way Jacob lived his life, we can't help but notice an eeriness as Joseph and his sons walk out the door. Could it be that Manasseh and Ephraim were just being polite and wanted to play along with their dad's and crazy old grandfather's desires? After all, they were young, full of life, and had access to everything the world had to offer. In other words, there wasn't much they lacked. For instance, they both had an impressive pedigree in that their father had extraordinary influence in Egypt and their mother was the daughter of Potiphera, priest of On. Both were around the age of twenty and ready to take on the world. Both could expect to be placed in high profile jobs with great pay and benefits. Both, most likely, were on Egypt's top ten most eligible bachelors' list. In short, things were good, the future was nothing but bright, and both were set for life.

Therefore, many would consider it reasonable to ask, "With all this prestige and promise, why were they so submissive to Jacob, a one hundred and thirty year old man on his deathbed?" Some would think that after Jacob finished blessing them the boys had every right to look up and say, "Thanks granddad but no thanks! We like where our future is heading here in Egypt." Others would argue that as Jacob finished his speech Manasseh should have stood up and said, "What! Are you kidding me? My little brother is going to be getting more than I am, and you think he will be better than me?" From a materialistic view, who could blame them? However, as we know, none of that happened. Instead, during all the pleasantries the boys were mannerly and honoring. Joseph's sons were obedient to every request their father and grandfather made. They stood where asked to stand and bowed when asked to bow. In other words, they were the spitting image of their father as they received Jacob's blessing with silent gratitude.

Were Manasseh and Ephraim just being nice and putting up a front so their father and grandfather would be happy? No, not at all. Based on the later prosperity of their tribes and their descendants' involvement in the Promised Land Relocation Project, their reaction toward their grandfather was from the heart. However, we're still left wondering, "What made the difference in his bedroom that day?" As impressive as Ephraim's and Manasseh's actions were, the real difference was made by the people who daily made the most of every teaching moment and invested themselves into their son's lives... and that, of course, would be their parents. Mom and Dad raised their sons in a home that showed them how to trust a sovereign God, displayed how to put others first, and taught a deep love for family.

Every morning, as the boys were growing up, it's possible that Joseph, Asenath, Manasseh, and Ephraim would gather around the breakfast table before their dad headed off to work. During the meal, Joseph would have had numerous opportunities to intentionally invest in his sons by telling them countless stories from his childhood and adolescent years. There would have been no end to the tales Joseph could have told about his despair and his triumphs, his dungeons and his dreams, his rejections and his promotions, and his losses and his gains. But through all his ups and downs, Joseph would have been able to weave a golden thread of God's sovereignty throughout each account. He could confidently tell his family how the Lord perfectly designed each scenario to get him to Egypt. Joseph could tell how his journey was to fulfill God's plan to ultimately save him, his family, and the entire world from starvation. Manasseh and Ephraim had to have been hanging on every word as their father described how the Heavenly Father graciously protected him in every situation. With great joy Joseph could have shared with his sons how he trusted the Sovereign God throughout his entire life and that they could trust the Lord with their lives too. That's one reason why it can be said that as Manasseh and Ephraim were receiving the blessing from their grandfather they were well aware of the Sovereignty of

God and that they could trust Him with their future.

Lunchtime must have been the highlight of the day for Joseph's family. When he was able to escape for an hour or two from saving the world, he could have come home to take a break from his busy schedule and visit the people he loved most. As soon as Joseph hit the door, Manasseh and Ephraim must have made a beeline straight for their daddy to knock him down and cover him with hugs and kisses. It must have been a festive time for Asenath and Joseph, while the boys were little, to spend some time together surrounded with great food and family. Nowhere in God's Word describes how joyous the family mealtime was at Joseph's house more than when he invited all his brothers over for lunch. Let's revisit this story but this time let's focus on things from a different angle.

Joseph's brothers had just returned for a second time to Egypt. This time, however, they were accompanied by their youngest brother Benjamin. Shortly after they had arrived, Joseph invited his siblings over to his house for lunch. Joseph, the consummate host, told his personal steward, "Take these men to my house, slaughter an animal and prepare a meal; they are to eat with me at noon" (Genesis 43:16). As the meal began, the brothers knew they were in for a treat. Being honored guests in the home of a high-ranking Egyptian official was not a bad place to be. But something strange happened when the food began to be served. The Bible says, "When portions were served to them from Joseph's table, Benjamin's portion was five times as much as anyone else's" (Genesis 43:34). While they were eating, the extra helpings for little brother must have peaked their curiosity, especially since it was so much more than everyone else's.

Therefore, we are left with the question: why the number five? Of course Joseph was again testing his brother's envious attitudes but why not two or ten? Where did the number five come from? It has been speculated that the extra portions on Benjamin's plate came from the plates of the host family. It's believed that Joseph, Asenath, Manasseh, and Ephraim each graciously gave their servings to this one man out of the eleven. Joseph and Asenath saw an opportunity to be generous toward Benjamin and, at the same time, teach their boys how to be selfless. This simple act of giving would have taught their sons how easy it is to put others first. With that, it can be said that as Manasseh and Ephraim were receiving the blessing from their grandfather they knew how to put others ahead of themselves.

Not only did Joseph and Asenath show their sons how to trust a sovereign God and how to put others first, but they taught them to have a deep love for family as well. To show how deep Joseph's love was for his family we need to again return to the climax of the previous chapter.

We pickup the story at the point where Joseph was weeping uncontrollably. Judah had just given the speech of the century, and Joseph could no longer contain his emotions. At long last he saw that the Lord had truly changed the hearts of his brothers. As he regained his composure, Joseph knew he desperately wanted to be reunited with his entire family. He wasted no time in saying to his brothers, "Now hurry back to my father and say to him, 'This is what your son Joseph says: God has made me lord of all Egypt. Come down to me; don't delay. You shall live in the region of Goshen and be near me—you, your children and grandchildren, your flocks and herds, and all you have. I will provide for you there, because five years of famine are still to come'" (Genesis 45:9-11). Some news has the ability to travel at light speed. Joseph's loving outburst and lavish invitation to his bothers broke the sound barrier as it was heard throughout the city. This headline even made it to Pharaoh's house. Not to be outdone, "When the news reached Pharaoh's palace that Joseph's brothers had come, Pharaoh and all his officials were pleased. Pharaoh said to Joseph, 'Tell your brothers, do this: Load your animals and return to the land of Canaan, and bring your father and your families back to me. I will give you the best of the land of Egypt and you can enjoy the fat of the land'" (Genesis 45:16-18). They were having a party at Joseph's house!

In all the commotion, Manasseh and Ephraim must have been filled with curiosity and questions. With Joseph's outburst, then his outpouring of love for his brothers, the boys would have seen firsthand the importance their dad put on family. As inquiring as most boys tend to be, Joseph would have had numerous opportunities as they sat at home to answer their questions about what led him to reveal himself to his brothers. He could have shared with his sons how he was able to forgive his brothers of the terrible things they did to him in the past. Just before bedtime, Joseph could have talked about how the Lord gave him wisdom to systematically test his brothers before he would reveal himself. But perhaps more importantly, Joseph could have explained how the Lord had given him discernment to see the transformation that had taken place in his brothers' hearts. The boys, without a doubt, would have understood their dad's heart. They would have definitely seen how he loved his family and how desperately he wanted to be reunited with them. Again, we see why it can be said that as Manasseh and Ephraim were receiving the blessing from their grandfather they were expressing a genuine love for their family too.

Joseph and Asenath raised their sons in a home that showed them how to trust a sovereign God, displayed how to put others first, and taught a deep love for family. Obviously, these life-lessons had firmly taken root in Manasseh's and Ephraim's lives, and this was never more evident than when they were in Jacob's bedroom receiving God's promised blessing. Just like Joseph and Asenath, the Lord gives parents many opportunities throughout each day to be intentional with their children. Whether it be during a meal, while sitting around the house, driving down the road, or just before bedtime, parents can take advantage of these moments to invest in their children's lives. When parents engage in spiritual conversations with their children, it has the potential to open the door for the Lord to capture their hearts and completely transform their lives.

LET'S GET PRACTICAL
Pastor Mark Holmen

What this portion of our story illustrates is the significant role parents play in the spiritual formation of their children. As an author who has written eight Christian parenting books I am frequently asked, "What is the key thing parents need to do to pass on the Christian faith to their children and children's children?" My answer is simply this: live in love with God by walking the walk and talking the talk. Essentially, do what Joseph did! Let's examine these ideas one at time.

Live in love with God. Your children are going to love who and what you love, so if you want your children to love God, then you need to love God. If you want them to love worship and church, then you need to love worship and the church. If you want them to love the Word of God, then you need to love the Word of God. And if you want them to love others as Christ loves us, then you need to love others as Christ loves us. I was co-leading a workshop at a parenting conference, and the other presenter began by asking the parents, "How many of you want your children to have a stronger relationship with Jesus Christ?" Pretty much every hand went up. Then he dropped the bomb, "Realize that what you are seeing in your child's faith is a mirror image of your faith." While I thought people would be angry with him, instead they all nodded in agreement because they knew he was speaking the truth. Joseph loved the Lord with all his heart, soul and strength, and as a result he had children who naturally did the same. And in case you think you have blown it and that it's too late because you haven't loved the Lord the way you should, please know that we serve a God of second chances (Praise the Lord!) Our children are continually watching us and being influenced by the way

113

we live our lives. So when you make the change to start living in love with Christ, your kids will notice and it will influence them.

Secondly we need to walk the walk which simply means we need to take our faithfulness with us wherever we go. In other words, we remain Christ-followers at work, in the car, in our neighborhoods and wherever God leads us to go. You don't ever "check out" of living your life by following the ways of God. That is another thing Joseph did better than most people. He had all sorts of opportunities to not follow God's ways, but he didn't waver and that impressed his kids. If you want to impress faith on your kids, you need to show them what it looks like to walk in the ways of Christ at all times and in all situations. When you do this, it will set an example for them to follow.

And finally, we need to talk the talk which simply means we need to share our faith journey with our children verbally. They need to hear our story with our ups and downs because God has given us that story for a reason. No story is perfect, but every story is unique. You have a unique story and God has had you on a unique journey. Your children need to know that story. Talking the talk does not mean having all the answers or knowing everything the Bible has to say. If it did, I would be in big trouble! Our children need to hear the story from us and not just from the professionals at church. What we say and how we say it is more influential than anything the church can say no matter how well they do it. Joseph shared his up-and-down journey through life with his children, and he shared how God lead him through that journey. That story left an impression on his children. Your God-story and God-journey will do the same, so trust in it. Talk continually to your children about what God is doing and has done in your life.

LET'S TALK

Here are some questions I would like you to ponder and/or discuss:

1. How well do you live in love with Christ? Would your children say you are in love with Christ? Who is someone you know that you would say is absolutely "in love" with Christ? How does their love for Christ impact or influence you?

2. How well do you walk the walk? Where do you find it easy to do life God's way and where do you find it difficult?

3. How well do you talk the talk? Do you find it easy or difficult to talk to your children about God and his ways?

4. As you reflect on your journey through life, how have you seen God at work? Have you told your children these things?

CONFLICT RESOLUTION
Dr. Mark Smith

This was a sad but expected occasion for the family of Jacob. In light of their father's physical condition, they knew it was only a matter of time before he would be departing his earthly home. But before he would breathe his last, Jacob still had some unfinished business to attend to. The Bible says, "Then Jacob called for his sons and said: 'Gather around so I can tell you what will happen to you in days to come. Assemble and listen, sons of Jacob; listen to your father Israel'" (Genesis 49:1-2). As the boys gathered and leaned in together to hear their father's last words, they must have had mixed emotions. Filled with sorrow, these men were eager to hear what high values and special futures their dad would pronounce over their lives. For many of Jacob's sons, they would not leave their father's house disappointed. He would indeed speak God's bountiful blessings not only into their lives but also in the lives of their future descendants. However, there would be those who would not fare so well. One son in particular would receive his father's blessing, but unfortunately his words would also include his discipline. Reuben was that son. Reuben's poor decision-making and lack of self-confidence led Jacob to add his correction as he spoke to his oldest son.

Perhaps to better understand the situation we need to listen in on the last words Jacob spoke to Reuben in front of all his brothers. It was there that Jacob said, "Reuben, you are my firstborn, my might and the beginning of my strength, the excellency of dignity and the excellency of power. Unstable as water, you shall not excel, because you went up to your father's bed; Then you defiled it—He went up to my couch" (Genesis 49:3-4). As we can see, Jacob did speak some encouragement into Reuben's life, but he also had some rather surprising things to say. Was Reuben getting a bad rap or was Jacob speaking truth? To decide, we need to rewind the clock a few years to see if we can shed any light on what caused Jacob to speak so bluntly.

To begin, let's go back to when Reuben was a young man in his twenties. At the time he had ten brothers and a sister. His stepmother, Rachel, was pregnant with her second child. His family was making their way from their worship celebration in Bethel to a new location on the outskirts of Migdal Eder. While the family was in transit, Rachel's baby would wait no longer. It was time. Delivering a child is traumatic as it is, but to be giving birth on the road must have added to the trauma. Scripture tells us that because of her difficulty in child-bearing Rachel lost her life, and Jacob buried her in the town we know today as Bethlehem.

This was a difficult time in Jacob's life. Losing his favorite wife, Rachel, was heartbreaking. The love of his life was gone. But God had mercy. At the ripe old age of around one hundred years the Lord gave Jacob his twelfth son. With mixed emotions the family moved on to their new home.

As Jacob and his family were getting settled and adjusting to a new way of life, the unthinkable happened. The Bible says, "While Israel was living in that region, Reuben went in and slept with his father's concubine Bilhah, and Israel heard of it" (Genesis 35:22). In the middle of his grief, Jacob now had salt rubbed in a very deep wound.

118

His oldest son, his firstborn, the heir to the Abrahamic covenant had committed a heinous sin. Reuben had brought shame to his name, and as a result disqualified himself from the birthright and patriarchal blessing that Jacob would have naturally passed down to his firstborn son.

From a parent's perspective it is hard to discern what is more disheartening in this Genesis account: Reuben's sin of adultery or Jacob's speechlessness. When we consider Reuben's point of view, we wonder what was going through his mind? Why would he commit such an ungodly act? Was he crazy or did someone put him up to it? Some commentators suggest that Reuben was attempting to usurp his father's position and authority by using a pagan custom of forcefully taking charge of his concubines. Others say that as he was growing up he and Bilhah had affections for one another, and the time was right for their passionate interlude. However, there is one speculation that holds a bit more merit. Because of the love and loyalty he had for his mother, Reuben would sacrifice his own reputation and future for her happiness. Reuben knew that if he slept with Bilhah, Jacob would never lay with her again. This one action would improve Leah's chances of having sexual relations with Jacob because there were now only two women for him to choose from: Leah and Zilpah. These ideas certainly are plausible, but Scripture does not let us know for sure what Reuben's motives were. Nonetheless, Reuben had made a poor decision that he would pay for the rest of his life.

On the other hand we have to ask the same question of Jacob. After the disaster at Shechem, the need to relocate his family to Bethel then eventually to Migdal Eder, and the loss of his most loved wife Rachel, what was going through his mind? Life had been very difficult for Jacob lately. Now, to make matters worse, his oldest son had done the inconceivable. Having sex with Bilhah permanently severed the last connection he would have with his cherished wife Rachel. How would Jacob respond to Reuben? At this point in Genesis we are not given a single clue because Jacob had nothing to say. We are left only with his silence. Was he silent because the grief was more than he could bear? Was the shock of the situation too overwhelming? Was the disappointment so debilitating he could not utter a single word? Perhaps it was the opposite. Jacob may have sat back, looked at all that was happening in his family, and decided that no words could properly express what he wanted to say. Was it despair or wisdom? Whatever the case, one thing is certain: Reuben's and Jacob's relationship was in trouble, and as we will see, their conflict will only intensify.

Several years go by and our next encounter with Reuben seems to have him focusing his efforts on reconciling with his father, but this endeavor is regrettably one- sided. The scene has our fallen son of Jacob deep in negotiations with his brothers over the fate of one they call "that dreamer." Joseph, as we know, had recently made several poor decisions of his own with his brothers. Nine out of the ten brothers were ready to make permanent plans to remove him from the planet and send him to an early grave. They all wanted him dead... all except Reuben. As the brothers saw Joseph approaching, they were ready to execute their plan. It was then that Reuben stepped in to reason with his irate siblings and was able to convince them to reconsider. Reuben persuaded them by saying, "Let's not take his life" (Genesis 37:21b), he said. "Don't shed any blood. Throw him into this cistern here in the wilderness, but don't lay a hand on him"

(Genesis 37:22a). Reuben's brothers all complied, and as soon as Joseph got within reach they nabbed him, ripped off his coat, and tossed him into a deep, waterless hole. As they executed Reuben's plan, they were unaware that he had ulterior motives. Scripture adds, "Reuben said this to rescue him from them and take him back to his father" (Genesis 37:22b).

We have to hand it to Reuben. It seemed to be an admirable plan. It had the potential of returning him back into good graces with his father; however, there was some risk involved. Knowing his brothers and how much they hated Joseph, this could have easily backfired on him. If Reuben had brought Joseph back home and his father had somehow been informed of their evil intentions, there could have been grave consequences for our brave rescuer. Reuben was willing to take that chance even if it meant troubles down the road. But that's not how God allowed it to play out.

With Joseph quietly trapped in his cylindrical cell, the brothers sat down to enjoy a celebratory meal. But Reuben, for some insane reason, decided not to join them. He excused himself and left Joseph in the cistern with his bloodthirsty brothers in charge. Then without Reuben's consent, Judah saw an opportunity to make a little cash and sold Joseph to a group of passing gipsies. In one fell swoop, Reuben's restitution was short-circuited, resulting in a failed attempt to get back in good with dad.

There are some questions that need to be asked. Why did he not, as the oldest brother, stand up to his younger siblings and tell them, 'No! You are not going to lay a finger on him?' Why did Reuben leave Joseph with nine men having murderous aspirations and not stay to protect him? Was he afraid his brothers would discover his hidden agenda and thwart his plan? Maybe Jacob was right after all. We see evidence that when confronted with hard issues, Reuben made poor decisions and lacked self- confidence. Even though he did make an attempt to gain some part of his father's favor back, sadly Reuben could not win for losing.

Many years would pass before Reuben's name is mentioned in Scripture again. Later, in the book of Genesis, we find Reuben standing-with several of his brothers talking to Jacob. You recall that there was a severe famine in the land and their food supplies had been depleted. Reuben and his brothers had recently returned from a long journey to Egypt to buy grain for their families. They were able to bring back an ample supply of grain, but they encountered one slight problem. Reuben and his brothers had to come back home and face daddy one brother short. Jacob listened carefully as his sons gave their report of what transpired in Egypt with the man who was "lord over the land." Everything was making sense to their father until they told Jacob why they had to leave Simeon behind. The governor of Egypt had accused them of being spies and was holding Simeon hostage until they could prove their claim of "being honest men." To prove their innocence and free Simeon, Egypt's governor demanded they bring back their youngest brother, Benjamin. This is where Jacob came unglued and said, "You have deprived me of my children. Joseph is no more and Simeon is no more, and now you want to take Benjamin. Everything is against me" (Genesis 42:36)! At this Reuben spoke up and tried to offer a solution to his distraught father's predicament. He said, "You may put both of my sons to death if I do not bring him back to you. Entrust him to my care, and I will bring him back" (Genesis 42:37).

In that moment I'm sure you could have heard a pin drop. Everyone in the room, except Reuben, must have been dumbfounded by his words. Reuben had really stuck his foot squarely into his mouth. How could he say such a thing? Why was he so willing to sacrifice his own children but not harm any hairs on his own head? The man of the hour really strikes out with Jacob on this one. No way would Jacob entertain the thought of losing Benjamin or his grandsons. This event helps us understand Jacob's words a little more clearly. Apparently he knew what he was talking about when he told Reuben you are, "Unstable as water, you shall not excel" (Genesis 49:3a).

When we look back across Reuben's life we see a story of what could have been. He had a long impressive pedigree. He arrived into Jacob's family with a silver spoon in his mouth. The first great-grandson of the patriarch Abraham would be the only child, in a long list of brothers, to receive the coveted family blessing and a double portion of the family inheritance. Unfortunately, this thoroughbred kept stumbling out of the gate. Reuben was never able to get any traction and sadly seemed to limp through life. Reuben's life was a downward spiral into obscurity with each passing year. It's unimaginable how he must have felt that day when he was standing with his brothers hearing his father's words of discipline. After Jacob finished speaking, Reuben walked away from his father's bedside and was never heard from again, a man downcast and dejected. But perhaps the saddest part of all is that Jacob never made any effort to reconcile with Reuben or restore him. Their conflict was never resolved.

LET'S GET PRACTICAL
Pastor Mark Holmen

Everybody has an opinion today about pretty much everything. We have opinions regarding politics, sexual orientation, movies, Hollywood, organized religion, music as well as parenting. And behind every opinion is a perspective that has been shaped and molded by personal experiences. As you see in the story of Reuben, everyone has an opinion, yet every opinion is from an experience that has been shaped by personal experiences. Reuben's opinions, and therefore actions, are coming from his perspective as the first-born son who has a lot of additional pressure and expectation thrust upon him. He has a myriad of personal experiences that help us understand where he is coming from. The same could be said of his brothers as well as Joseph and Jacob. So what we are encountering in this story is a large family with a large number of opinions and perspectives that have each been shaped by personal experiences and surprise, surprise...they aren't all the same! And this all leads to conflict which could be the theme of this portion of the story. Conflict is a result of differing opinions over how to handle different situations, and everyone's opinion is coming from a perspective that is shaped by personal experience.

If you have a family, you have differing opinions which produce conflict. There is absolutely no way around it. The family you grew up in has conflict as a result of differing opinions, and I'm sure I could get a huge "AMEN!" to that statement! So the question becomes: how do we handle conflict in families, because like Reuben and his family showed us, conflict exists in all families? Let me provide a personal acronym which I hope will help you and your family address conflict.

C = Care

Show You Care

The best starting point in resolving conflict is to show how much you care. As the famous line goes, "They will not care how much you know until they know how much you care." Instead of trying to make/win your point/perspective, seek to win the "care" battle. Are you caring more about them and truly understanding their opinion and/or perspective or are you simply trying to get your point across? Showing you care will open the doors for better communication to occur.

O = Open

Stay Open

Are you open to other perspectives, opinions and experiences? Resolving conflict involves creating an environment of openness where everyone can share without feeling like they will be ridiculed or ostracized for their opinion.

N = Neutral

Remain Neutral or Engage A Neutral Party

For as long as possible, remain as neutral as possible allowing for all perspectives and opinions to be changed. Try to remain as neutral as possible for as long as possible before rendering your opinion or perspective. And if necessary, because everyone in the family is too engaged to be neutral, bring in a neutral party who can help you navigate your way through the conflict.

F = Focus

Stay Focused

When resolving conflict, one of the best things you can do is to continually focus and refocus your attention on the specific cause of the conflict and not stray away from that. You will need to continually ask, "What is the cause of our conflict and are we still focused on that?"

L = Listen

Listen More Than You Speak

Are you creating an environment where everyone is truly listening to one another? God gave us two ears and one mouth for a purpose so that we could listen twice as much as we speak!

I = Interpret

Interpretation Matters

Make sure all perspectives are understood. Simply ask, "Does everyone understand?" If not, spend additional time by asking, "Could you help us understand what you meant when...?" Clarity clears up a lot of conflict.

C = Compliment & Correct

Compliment & Correct Helps Diffuse the Situation

In a conflict situation seek to compliment new perspectives or healthy behaviors as much or more than you correct inaccuracies or poor behavior. Complimenting someone on what they shared or how they handled themselves can serve to diffuse many tense feelings. When needing to correct, soften it by phrasing it as a question, "Am I correct in saying...Is it accurate to say...?"

T = Time

It Takes Time

Not all conflicts can be resolved quickly. In many cases, the best healer is time allowing for people to calm down, rethink and process the things that have been said and done.

LET'S TALK

Here are some questions I would like you to ponder and/or discuss:

1. With whom in your family do you have a CONFLICT?

2. When it comes to CONFLICT, what is God's desire between you and the other person?

3. When it comes to CONFLICT, are you a good listener?

4. What is keeping you from seeking resolution from your CONFLICT?

5. Like Jacob, allow me to be blunt. Are you willing to let CONFLICT continue between you and your loved one knowing that life is short?

HOPE
Dr. Mark Smith

Without a doubt, Jacob and his family have my vote to be listed in the top 10 most dysfunctional families of the Bible. In each chapter, we saw firsthand how the caustic atmosphere of their home produced great tensions among family members. The entire family had poor communication skills and major obedience issues when it came to God's desires. Very few of them knew how to deal well with conflict nor did they know how to plan properly for the future. One person in particular was a manipulator, a workaholic, a coward and showed an extraordinary amount of favoritism which consistently led to disaster for everyone involved. Sadly, these issues didn't just stay in the unfriendly confines of their home. This family was an equal opportunity bedlam distributer who didn't seem to care if they drug others in and through their chaotic mess.

In many ways, Jacob's life was an incredible story of how to get through life the hard way. As a matter of fact, he said it himself when he told Pharaoh, "The years of my pilgrimage are a hundred and thirty. My years have been few and difficult..." (Genesis 47:9). Compared to today's standards, Jacob didn't have a short life, but it certainly was difficult. With the amount of turmoil that circulated in his home, I'm sure he endured countless nights when he would lay his head on the pillow and wish that the hopelessness would go away. If we are truly honest with ourselves, there are times when our current journey may not look much different than his. That's why I am so thankful that we have these stories, and many others like them in the Bible to help us see ourselves a little more clearly. But it is not enough that we only see ourselves in the characters of Scripture. The Lord longs for us to take the hope of His Word, apply it to every aspect of our lives, and live it out among our family and community.

When we need hope we can find it in passages of the Bible like these:

"For whatever was written in former days was written for our instruction, that through endurance and through the encouragement of the Scriptures we might have hope."
Romans 15:4

"Keep this Book of the Law always on your lips; meditate on it day and night, so that you may be careful to do everything written in it. Then you will be prosperous and successful."
Joshua 1:8

"Trust in the LORD and do good; dwell in the land and enjoy safe pasture. Take delight in the LORD, and he will give you the desires of your heart. Commit your way to the LORD; trust in him and he will do this: He will make your righteous reward shine like the dawn, your vindication like the noonday sun."
Psalm 37:3-6

"Follow God's example, therefore, as dearly loved children..."
Ephesians 5:1

"The righteous man walks in his integrity; His children are blessed after him." Proverbs 20:7

"Trust in the LORD with all your heart and lean not on your own understanding; in all your ways submit to him, and he will make your paths straight."
Proverbs 3:5-6

"I will give you a new heart and put a new spirit within you; I will take the heart of stone out of your flesh and give you a heart of flesh. I will put My Spirit within you and cause you to walk in My statutes, and you will keep My judgments and do them. Then you shall dwell in the land that I gave to your fathers; you shall be My people, and I will be your God. I will deliver you from all your uncleanness."
Ezekiel 36:26-29

"Blessed is the one who does not walk in step with the wicked or stand in the way that sinners take or sit in the company of mockers, but whose delight is in the law of the LORD, and who meditates on his law day and night. That person is like a tree planted by streams of water, which yields its fruit in season and whose leaf does not wither—whatever they do prospers."
Psalm 1:1-3

"When your words came, I ate them; they were my joy and my heart's delight, for I bear your name, LORD God Almighty."
Jeremiah 15:16

"I have told you these things, so that in me you may have peace. In this world you will have trouble. But take heart! I have overcome the world."
John 16:33

"The house of the wicked will be overthrown, but the tent (dwelling place, household) of the upright will flourish."
Proverbs 14:11

"Whoever dwells in the shelter of the Most High will rest in the shadow of the Almighty. I will say of the LORD, 'He is my refuge and my fortress, my God, in whom I trust.' Surely he will save you from the fowler's snare and from the deadly pestilence. He will cover you with his feathers, and under his wings you will find refuge; his faithfulness will be your shield and rampart. You will not fear the terror of night, nor the arrow that flies by day, nor the pestilence that stalks in the darkness, nor the plague that destroys at midday. A thousand may fall at your side, ten thousand at your right hand, but it will not come near you. You will only observe with your eyes and see the punishment of the wicked. If you say, 'The LORD is my refuge,' and you make the Most High your dwelling, no harm will overtake you, no disaster will come near your tent. For he will command his angels concerning you to guard you in all your ways; they will lift you up in their hands, so that you will not strike your foot against a stone. You will tread on the lion and the cobra; you will trample the great lion and the serpent. 'Because he loves me,' says the LORD, 'I will rescue him; I will protect him, for he acknowledges my name. He will call on me, and I will answer him; I will be with him in trouble, I will deliver him and honor him. With long life I will satisfy him and show him my salvation.'"
Psalm 91:1-16

"'For I know the plans I have for you,' declares the LORD, 'plans to prosper you and not to harm you, plans to give you hope and a future. Then you will call on me and come and pray to me, and I will

listen to you. You will seek me and find me when you seek me with all your heart.'"
Jeremiah 29:11-13

"The LORD is my light and my salvation—whom shall I fear? The LORD is the stronghold of my life—of whom shall I be afraid?"
Psalm 27:1

"...in all these things we are more than conquerors through him who loved us. For I am convinced that neither death nor life, neither angels nor demons, neither the present nor the future, nor any powers, neither height nor depth, nor anything else in all creation, will be able to separate us from the love of God that is in Christ Jesus our Lord."
Romans 8:37-39

"The LORD is good, a refuge in times of trouble. He cares for those who trust in him..."
Nahum 1:7

"Praise the LORD, my soul, and forget not all his benefits— who forgives all your sins and heals all your diseases, who redeems your life from the pit and crowns you with love and compassion..."
Psalm 103:2-4

"Set your minds on things above, not on earthly things."
Colossians 3:2

"If I rise on the wings of the dawn, if I settle on the far side of the sea, even there your hand will guide me, your right hand will hold me fast."
Psalm 139:9-10

"Cast your cares on the LORD and he will sustain you; he will never let the righteous be shaken."
Psalm 55:22

"What, then, shall we say in response to these things? If God is for us, who can be against us?"
Romans 8:31

"Do not repay anyone evil for evil. Be careful to do what is right in the eyes of everyone. If it is possible, as far as it depends on you, live at peace with everyone."
Romans 12:17-18

"Many are the woes of the wicked, but the LORD's unfailing love surrounds the one who trusts in him. Rejoice in the LORD and be glad, you righteous; sing, all you who are upright in heart!"
Psalm 32:10-11

"Be still, and know that I am God; I will be exalted among the nations, I will be exalted in the earth."
Psalm 46:10

In these verses hope abounds for all of us. God has made sure that Jacob, and many others like him in Scripture, have a voice in our lives today so that we don't have to repeat the same mistakes tomorrow. However, if we do make similar mistakes, the Lord assures us He is always there for his children. Regardless of your situation, there is always hope. Always!

ABOUT THE AUTHORS

Dr. Mark Smith and his high school sweetheart, Sherri, have been married since 1987. The Lord has blessed them with four wonderful children Abby and her husband Justus and Adam and his wife Ashlynn. Mark has served in student ministry for over twenty years and is currently serving as Family Pastor at Lakeview Baptist Church in Hickory, North Carolina. Dr. Smith graduated from North Carolina State University in engineering, Southeastern Baptist Theological Seminary with a Master of Divinity, and Liberty Baptist Theological Seminary with a Doctorate of Ministry and is the author of Parental Guidance Suggested.

Pastor Mark A. Holmen is the Executive Director of Faith@Home Ministries which equips congregations and families to establish the home as the primary place where faith is lived and nurtured (www.faithathome.com). Pastor Mark has served as a Sr. Pastor as well as youth and family pastor and has authored numerous books including his popular Faith Begins@Home series of booklets as well as Impress Faith on Your Kids and Church + Home: Pastor Holmen is a nationally and internationally recognized speaker and seminar leader who has spoken for Focus On The Family, Family Life, D6, and the Willow Creek Association. Pastor Mark and his wife, Maria, have been married for 24 years and have a daughter Malyn.